THE HINDU CASTE SYSTEM
Volume 1
THE SACRALIZATION OF A SOCIAL ORDER

The Hindu Caste System
Volume 1
THE SACRALIZATION OF A SOCIAL ORDER

HAROLD A. GOULD

Chanakya Publications
Delhi

ISBN: 81-7001-023-3

THE HINDU CASTE SYSTEM, Vol. 1
The Sacralization of a Social Order
by
HAROLD A. GOULD

Copyright © 1987 Harold A. Gould

First published 1987
by
CHANAKYA PUBLICATIONS
F 10/14 Model Town, Delhi 110009

Reprinted 1990

Printed in India
at
PRESSWORKS, 1813, Chandrawal Road Delhi 110007

Preface

This book contains five essays on the caste system of India that were written and published in various places over the last eighteen years. I have added an introductory chapter which I hope will give the reader an integrated picture of the contemporary state of my thinking on the subject. Although each paper in the collection was written to stand on its own, I believe that in their severalty they complement one another both as to their conceptual orientation and the empirical aspects of caste with which they respectively deal. "Caste and Class. . . . (Chapter Two) and the "Introduction" (Chapter 1) address the issue of where the caste system fits into the scheme of preindustrial social stratification. Chapter Two, in addition, compares the organizational principles of preindustrial social stratification with modern forms of social stratification. Chapters Three and Four ("Castes, Outcastes..." and "Priest and Contrapriest...") each in their own way address the question of what social and cultural mechanisms were involved in the diffusion of pan-Indian caste both within the Indian sub-continent and beyond its geographical frontiers. The final two chapters on the Hindu *jajmani* system (". . . A Case of Economic Particularism" and ". . . Its Structure, Magnitude and Meaning") provide empirical and analytical insights into how caste organizes social interaction in accordance with Hindu values in on-going rural communities.

Over the many years during which the research and living that lies behind this book was taking place, there have been many individuals and institutions whose generosity, encouragement and friendship have made the final result possible. Between 1954 and the present, my work in India has been facilitated by grants from the Fulbright Foundation (1954-55), the National

Science Foundation (1959-60), the National Institute of Mental Health (1960-62), The American Institute of Indian Studies (1966-67, 1974, 1975, 1981-82), the Smithsonian Institution (1980, 1984), and the University of Illinois (1970, 1975). Within India itself debts of gratitude for help and support are owed to the Department of Anthropology of Lucknow University, the Institute of Economic Growth at Delhi University and the Center for the Study of Developing Societies in Delhi.

The number of individuals who over the years have made my work possible and my life livable in India would fill a separate volume if I attempted to name them all. But no such list could leave off the following persons: the special intellectual brotherhood and more than thirty years of unbroken friendship with Dr. T.N. Madan of the Institute of Economic Growth with whose family our family became one. This would include, of course, Shiv and Mira Ram whose loving care transformed me into a 'Delhi-walla'! The late D.N. Majumdar, the founder of Anthropology at Lucknow University, who guided my initial passage to India during my days as a struggling graduate student. Ram Advani, Bookseller of Lucknow, whose friendship is special and spans the entire period that India and I have been part of each other. The people of Birauly, the real name of the village in Faizabad district in which I lived and worked during the early years. Especially Thakur Ram Babhuti Singh, Ram Chunder Yaduv, Surye and Badal Das. In Faizabad-*cum*-Ayodhya, the district capital, Ram Harakh Singh ('the American master'), Brij Nandan Prasad, the late Suraj Pal Singh of Janaura, the late Babu Priyadatta Ram and his son Jyotipat Ram. A special measure of acknowledgement and affection for Mr. Ram Krishna Pandey without whose help very little could have been accomplished in Faizabad district.

Finally, the list would be incomplete if it did not include near its top the name of Dr. P. Mehendirata, Indian Director of the American Institute of Indian Studies whose skills, leadership and enduring personal friendship over twenty years have formed an immeasurable part of my Indian experience.

In America, acknowledgements must begin with the late Professor Jules Henry, my mentor and my friend, who taught me the importance of caring for humanity as well as merely studying it. Thanks also to Professors Kurt H. Wolff (Brandeis University) and John W. Bennett (Washington University, St. Louis) for many lessons learned. And special thanks to Professor Richard A. Schermerhorn (Rtd.) who was there at the creation and substantially responsible for it. Finally special thanks to The Late Marge Hurder for monumental patience with me and many monotonous hours at the word processor.

Urbana
Oct. 1986

Harold A. Gould

Acknowledgements

Chapter Two *McCaleb Module in Anthropology*, Module 11 (1971); 1-24. Copyright (No. AA 305855, Dec. 1972) assigned to Harold A. Gould, June 6, 1979, Benjamin/Cummings Publishing Company.

Chapter Three Revised version of paper whose original was published by the *International Journal of Comparative Sociology*, Vol. 1 (1959): 222-238.

Chapter Four Reprinted with permission from *Contributions to Indian Sociology*, New Series, No. 1 (1967): 28-57.

Chapter Five Reprinted with permission from the *Journal of Anthropological Research* (formerly the *Southwestern Journal of Anthropology*, Vol. 14 (1958): 428-437.

Chapter Six Reprinted with permission from *Ethnology*, Vol. 3 (1964): 12-41

This book is dedicated to
KETY, *SHERU* AND *ARMEEN*
'The Home Team'

Contents

Preface v

Acknowledgements viii

1. Introduction: The Sacralization of a Social Order 1
2. Caste and Class: A Comparative View 29
3. Castes, Outcastes and Sociology of Stratification 73
4. Priests and Contrapriests: A Structural Analysis of Jajmani Relationships in the Hindu Plains and the Nilgiri Hills 103
5. The Hindu Jajmani System: A Case of Economic Particularism 135
6. A Jajmani System of North India: Its Structure, Magnitude and Meaning 149

Index 190

1

Introduction: The Sacralization of a Social Order

> ... what is there among Coorgs that is not Hindu? Nothing, because the Coorgs are Hindus. And they are Hindus essentially because they adhere to Hindu values.[1]

I have subtitled this collection of essays on the caste system 'the sacralization of a social order' as a way of stressing my conviction that this ancient social institution was the *necessary* sociological manifestation of the underlying moral-philosophical presuppositions of Hinduism. Without traditional Hinduism there could have been no caste system. Without the caste system traditional Hindu values would have been socially inexpressible. To this extent I find myself in the same camp with Louis Dumont and Edmund Leach. More than twenty-five years ago, Professor Leach (1960) asserted, in what has endured as a classic statement on the subject, that, "Caste, in my view, denotes a particular species of social organization indissolubly linked with what Dumont rightly insists is a pan-Indian civilization." (p. 5)[2]

To say that the caste system of India is a type of social organization which can exist solely within the ambit, and as a social manifestation, of pan-Indian civilization (which in this case means *Hindu* civilization) is not to say, however, that the broad principles or forms of social organization which underlay it were unique to the Indic world. Sociologically speaking, the caste system, its Hindu-ness notwithstanding, is a system of social stratification rooted in an occupationalized division of labor no different in its fundamental characteristics, *qua* social stratification, from that associated with all of the Old World high civilizations whose origins are traceable back to the technological revolutions which began in and on the peripheries of the Fertile Crescent ten or so milennia ago. This point is stressed in the first two essays of this collection.[3]

What I should like to do in this introductory essay is to review some of the arguments concerning the origins, development, functions and meaning of caste in India and try, in the process, to bring my own thinking on the subject into the picture. Clearly there has been a long debate in the literature over whether the caste system is a unique social phenomenon or simply one manifestation of processes of social stratification which have a wider generality.[4] The work of Dumont and Pocock,[5] Marriott and Inden,[6] and their students, the views of Leach, over the past two decades have stressed the element of uniqueness. That of Bailey,[7] Berreman,[8] Passin,[9] De Vos and Wagatsuma,[10] and perhaps Klass,[11] as well as my own,[12] have stressed the opposite perspective. In my opinion, the choice between these two positions is not an absolute one despite the often strident assertions to the contrary emanating from partisans of the one or the other. Whether the caste system is viewed from the standpoint of that which makes it indigenously Indian, and Hindu, or that which links it to what I have called ascription-oriented stratification (see Chapter Two) generally depends on what one chooses to emphasize.

Regardless of which side of the argument one chooses, there are certain characteristics of the caste system which are almost universally acknowledged to be associated with it as a sociocultural institution. One, of course, is its enormous longevity. Descriptions of caste are almost as old as recorded history itself. Greek scholars traveling with Alexander the Great in the 4th century BC not only commented on it but had themselves been made aware of its existence by the accounts of even earlier Greek adventurers associated with Persian expeditions into northwestern India.[13] Greeks subsequently connected with the Seleucid court and the Bactrian kingdoms that succeeded Alexander rendered accounts of it. So did Chinese-Buddhist pilgrims centuries later and European travelers during the mercantilist age.[14] British civil servants during the *Raj* wrote volumes on India's dominant social structure.[15] And what is remarkable of course is how consistent such descriptions were over more than two milennia. Everyone described a rigidly structured division of labor composed of hereditary, occupattionally specialized groups, the groups to which the term *jati* is indigenously applied. Most significantly it was universally perceived that a priestly class, the Brahmans, reposed at the apex of this hierarchical social structure and dominated it by the performance of rituals controlled exclusively by them and by practicing an ascetic life-style which decisively set them apart from other social groups in society. Finally, no one failed to remark on the Untouchables, the so-called 'outcastes,' a vast congeries of persons who were doomed by the polluting implications of the work they performed to live wretched existences at the nadir of the social order.

The task confronting all modern social scientists, social historians and others concerned with trying to make sense of the caste system has been to try and account for the persistence and viability of this most remarkable of all human institutions. The essays in this volume are one such attempt. Their purpose has been to demonstrate that the caste system represents a particular conjuncture between a pattern of religious values, *viz*, Hinduism, and a system of social stratification, the product of the technologies and political economies which Old World preindustrial, urban civilizations brought into being originally in the Fertile Crescent.

On what do we base the claim that the caste system of India is simultaneously a uniquely Hindu social institution and merely one variation of an extremely widespread species of social structure? The answer lies in making an analytical distinction between society and culture, something which Bailey (1959) was insisting on more than a quarter of a century ago in his critique of Dumont's and Pocock's call for a 'Sociology of India.' Recoiling from their emphasis on the indigenous (i.e., cultural) dimensions of caste to the virtual exclusion of all others he accuses them of making "an insufficiently rigorous distinction between cultural and social facts," (p. 97) of thereby making it impossible to undertake one of the most important things that scientific investigations are supposed to undertake—*viz*, make systematic comparisons. "What then becomes of comparative sociology?" Bailey exclaims. The comparative sociologist, after all, "wants to find out what India has in common with other societies..." (p. 97) For scholars who share these concerns :

> A definition of caste which rules out comparison with, for instance, the Southern States of America or even with South Africa, is useless for comparative sociology. (p.97).

Thus, he continues :

> What is distinctively Indian belongs to the particularistic disciplines of culture and history; sociology deals in systems and to my mind the Indian sociologist is a person who happens to have been born in India. There can be no "Indian" sociology except in a vague and geographic sense, any more than there are distinctively Indian principles in chemistry and biology. (p. 99)

What Bailey failed to make clear in the heat of his polemic, however, was that there *can be* a 'sociology of India' which stresses the specific interrelationships between social structures *in India* and the complex of cultural phenomena (moral and religious values, symbols, etc.) which are, in effect, Indian civilization. Put another way, he didn't adequately stress the fact that one can study the *use* to which social structure was put in the effort by the votaries of Hinduism to *express* their moral presuppositions in social terms. But Bailey does make an important observation in the course of his debate with Dumont and Pocock which points in the right direction. He alludes to S F. Nadel's point (1951) that 'society' is at a higher level of abstraction (i.e., is a more generally inclusive concept) than is 'culture.'[16] Applied to the relationship between the specific, culturally molded phenomenon, the *caste system*, it allows us to factor into our analyses the fact that 'society' whose division of labor and system of social stratification Hinduism made 'Indian' (i.e., a culturally specific manifestation of social organization) was compounded of basic interactional relationships and structural principles that applied far beyond India's borders and were products of processes universally characteristic of human societies at a certain stage of social evolution.

We must look back over the history of social scientific thinking about caste to appreciate how diverse have been the attempts even in modern times to comprehend its nature and how consistently such attempts have been shattered on the rocks of inadequate conceptualization. There are many references to this history in the ensuing essays. However, Dumont and Pocock in the early volumes of *Contributions to Indian Sociology* deserve credit for bringing systematic attention to bear on this babel. Through their reproduction of and commented summaries on the work of Celestin Bouglé, A.M. Hocart, M.N. Srinivas and others[17] they succeeded in demonstrating that understanding Indian society required something more than listing and describing hundreds or thousands (depending on how one differentiated them) of occupationally/ritually specialized social compartments into which Indian society resolved itself. It was, they realized, necessary to abstract from this vast and bewildering array of social differentia the key structural properties which they all shared. It was, in short, a matter of focussing not on castes *per se* but on a *system* of hereditary social compartments whose interrelationships were rendered predictable everywhere in India because they socially expressed cultural values which lay at the heart of India's dominant religious tradition. India is a case where a particular 'use' was made of the given 'social facts' of occupationalized work and stratified occupations. Dumont and Pocock refer to a statement by Srinivas which depicts this fundamental relationship between culture and social structure very clearly :

> The caste system has enabled a vast number of tiny groups with distinct cultures, occupations and systems of belief to live side by side, the autonomy of each being respected while at the same time cooperation was ensured between them. (p. 212)

One may put it that the caste system is part of a society, and the social expression of a religious system, which *caused* the "tiny groups" with "distinctive cultures, occupations and systems of belief," as Srinivas put it, "to live side by side" while being *functionally interdependent in both religious and economic terms*. Some of these groups got integrated into the *system* by "modifying their values" while others were created by the very logic of the caste system itself. 'Race' and 'nationality' were *transmuted* into the religious and economic categories of an intricate division of labor which served religious needs as crucially as purely economic and political needs. What was important was the *process* of 'transmutation,' something made possible by the enormous moral influence on the entire fabric of Indian society which an emergent class of religious specialists, the Brahmans, were able to exert.

Weber, Bouglé and later Hocart, each in their own way had grasped the fact that the caste system in India represented a remarkable manifestation of the interplay between social and cultural forces. This "unique social system," as Weber (1958) characterized it, "could not have originated or at least not have conquered and lasted without the powerful and all-pervasive influence of the Brahmans." (p. 131) The *cultural achievement* in India was "The specific Brahmanical theodicy" which Weber termed "a stroke of genius" because it was plainly "the construction of rational ethical thought" (a *cultural* process) and not the mechanical outgrowth or 'byproduct' (*a la* Marx) of economic determinism. This theodicy was the doctrine of *karma* which "combined" with "the empirical social order through the promise of rebirth." It sacralized the social order (to paraphrase Hocart) and thus "gave this social order the irresistable power over thought and hope of men embedded in this order and furnished the fixed schema for the *religious and social integration* of the various professional groups and pariah peoples." (p. 131. Emphasis is mine).

Like Weber, Celestin Bouglé saw that caste was a social structure which depended for its reality on the Brahmanic codes. It was the *systemic* nature of this phenomenon which set it apart from rigid forms of social stratification found elsewhere and this systemic quality arose from the Indian environment which nurtured it. Bouglé also believed that the Brahman, "by making himself worshipped," was a "special species" who functioned as the ritual focal point of the system. (p. 56) But he refused "to attribute the creation of the caste system to the interested calculation, artifices and conspiracies of Brahmans." In proper Durkheimian fashion, for Bouglé was a Durkheimian, he believed that it arose "from the occurrence of spontaneous and collective tendencies." (p. 60) These tendencies lay at its sociological heart and accounted for its "spirit" (i.e., its cultural singularity). They were: "repulsion, hierarchy and hereditary specialization." (p. 9) The most critical of the three from the cultural standpoint was "repulsion" which was the word he selected to stress the importance of 'pollution,' 'ritual pollution,' or 'purity-pollution ' Occupational groups were not only hereditary and arranged in a hierarchy, but because of Brahmanic religion their differences were *morally absolute* as well. Occupations had sacred significance, the separateness was moral, and their interdependence was therefore permanent and unalterable. The occupationally differentiated groups "repel each other," asserted Bouglé. (p. 9) The social stratification system "divides them not merely into superimposed levels but into a *multitude of opposed fragments*; it brings each of their *elementary groups face to face, separated by a mutual repulsion.*" (p. 9. Emphasis is mine.)

It was A.M. Hocart (1950), an early twentieth century thinker whose seminal scholarship did not surface until years after it had been originally undertaken, who demonstrated that a symbiotic relationship between the royal court and occupational specialists was the social structural focal point of the caste system. Unlike his predecessors who had worked almost exclusively from secondary sources, Hocart had lived, worked and conducted research in southern Asia and Polynesia. He had observed at first hand the operation of social stratification systems whose structure had been profoundly marked if not actually directly shaped by concepts of purity and pollution. Hocart concluded that the caste system is a 'sacrificial structure,' that the work performed by hereditary specialists (especially by certain specialists) is *necessary* to the *cultural existence* of Hindu society, and by extension Sinhalese society as well. "Crafts and rites are strictly distinguishable," says Hocart, "and the Sanskrit word *Karma*, 'deed,' 'work,' expresses both " (p. 16) The craftsman is more than an economic functionary, he is a ritual functionary as well. He "has the ear of the deity presiding over some particular activity." (p. 10) And the sociopolitical locus of this ritualized division of labor and system of social stratification is the monarch or his structural equivalent, for it is he who has the earthly power and resources to enforce the rules and embody the moral and religious values by which and for which it exists. Thus :

> The conclusion we have arrived at on modern evidence is that the caste system is a sacrificial organization, that the aristorcracy are feudal lords constantly involved in rites for which they require vassals or serfs, because some of these services involve pollution from which the lord must remain free. (p. 17)

Hocart's terminology was still archaic by contemporary standards. But what he was already clearly depicting, of course, was the basic logic of the *jajmani* system, the interactional basis of the caste system. The *jajmani* system is the caste system viewed from the standpoint of the day-to-day interactions through which religious values are economically expressed and economic behavior is invested with religious meaning. It is with this aspect of the caste system that the pioneering work of William Wiser (1936) dealt, with which many scholars have subsequently dealt,[18] and with which the last two papers in this volume deal. Hocart's analysis showed essentially that Indic religion, wherever it became established, transmuted the occupationalized division of labor into a complex sophisticated socioreligious structure which simultaneously performed economic and ritual functions. Indian religion, to reiterate, created a particular species of social stratification,--*viz*, the caste system.

One of Hocart's strengths, from our standpoint, was his comparativist perspective. Based on the breadth of his personal familiarity with southern Asian social phenomena, his thought flowed from an implicit understanding that the caste system had arisen from an ancient substratum of widely diffused preoccupation with magico-religious pollution[19] and was an historically specific conjuncture of culture and social structure within this domain. But equally valuable was Hocart's recognition of the importance of kingship and the royal court as the social context where political (i. e., secular) and supernatural power converge, comingle and produce the interactional model for caste structures at all levels of society. This was undoubtedly an insight which grew directly out of his geographic and consequent sociocultural perspective on the caste system. His principal vantage had been Ceylon and Buddhism rather than India and Hinduism. Sinhalese society was a variation on the theme. In Sinhalese society, as in Buddhist societies generally, royal and priestly power coterminated to a greater degree in the person of the king than was the case in Hindu society. The Brahman in India stood more vividly apart from and transcendant over all manifestations of secular authority because so much importance was attached to the fact that he was the master of ritual which sustained the cosmic order itself.

What the contrasting perspectives of Hocart, on the one hand, and Dumont and Pocock, on the other, made possible was the opportunity to isolate with greater clarity just what were the essential qualities inherent in kingship and priestship in the Indic world and to discern how these qualities were factored into the rituals which brought about the transformation of ordinary ascriptive social stratification into a system of caste interaction.

Through Hocart's studies from the Sinhalese perspective we see 'Brahmanic power' more encompassed by 'Kshatriya power' than in India but by no means completely merged with it. For to do so would be to liquidate the basis for ritual interaction between the *moral qualities* which Brahman and Kshatriya represent in the Indic world. We are thus able to see in the Sinhalese case, stripped of its essentials, what is one of the fundamental sociological ingredients of true caste systems—*viz*, political power requiring continuous ritual resanctification by priestly power. Despite Buddhism's rejection of orthodox Brahmanism, the *powers* and *functions* represented by the Brahmans are nevertheless integrally present in the ritual life of these courts. All have *purohits*, 'Brahmans,' whose roles are exclusively those of ritual specialists with few 'social carryovers,' as in India, extending beyond the courtly matrix, to resanctify the king, in other words, to 'manage' the pollution attendant upon the immersion in life process which must occur in the course of performing kingly duties.

Dumont and Pocock miss this important nuance where they down-play the comparabilities (ironically, at the sociological level of analysis which they champion!) between the Hindu caste system and that found in neighboring Ceylon. "Ceylon has all the characteristics of caste, except for its vigor," asserts Dumont in *Homo Hierarchicus* (1970). He continues :

> ...the king has remained the center both of group religion (as opposed to individualistic religion, the discipline of Buddhist salvation) and of political and economic life. We see therefore that the supremacy of the priest is an Indian fact which has remained unexportable: India has exported quasi-caste rather than caste proper...these countries know only the strictly royal 'liturgies' described by Hocart. (p. 216).

In a narrowly technical sense Dumont is correct when he says that the 'supremacy' of the priest was not exported to Ceylon or anywhere else where Buddhism took root. But it is important to realize that the ritually and religio-philosophically central aspects of the Brahman status *were* exported, especially to Celyon and Southeast Asia, and tended to produce there varyingly complex manifestations of Indic caste. In Ceylon the replication was highly detailed. In most of the major civilizations of Southeast Asia, with the Indianized royal courts acting as cultural loci, the *ideology* of caste was to be found even where the social structure itself was not. Bali is the most striking example, of course, but Java, Sumatra, Cambodia, Thailand and other early civilizations in the region also revealed social structural responses to the penetration of the Indic ritual mode.[20]

The difference in degree reflects the difference in structural, and consequently hierarchical separation, between the powers represented by priest and king in cultural worlds pervaded by concerns with the polluting implications of life-process. Dumont saw this in his essay on 'Kingship in Ancient India" written in 1962 for *Contributions to Indian Sociology* (No. 6). Comparing kingship in China and elsewhere in antiquity with the phenomenon in India, he says :

> in kingship of the Chinese empire. .the supreme religious functions were vested in the sovereign, he was the priest

par excellence and those who were called priests were only ritual specialists subordinate to him. Comparing this with the Indian situation, there seems to be a simple alternative: either the king exerts religious functions which are generally his, and then he is the head of the hierarchy for this very reason, and exerts at the same time political power, or, this is the Indian case, the king depends on the priests for the religious functions he cannot himself operate the sacrifice on behalf of the kingdom, instead he "puts in front" of himself a priest, the *purohita*, and then he loses the hierarchical preeminence in favor of the priests retaining for himself [political] power only. (pp 54-55)

The need for resanctification determines the need for this separation between priest and king, a need arising from the cultural triumph of the basic presuppositions about matter and substance, life and death, mortality and immortality in Indic religion. Maintaining social status (*varna* and *jati*) in the sentient world (*maya*) and ultimately overcoming mortal existence (*moksha*) requires a resanctifying priesthood whose rituals neutralize the polluting consequences of performing the mortal tasks (*karma*) ordained by the moral quality of previous births (*samsara*). Wherever and to whatever degree this ideological structure has diffused within India and to other parts of Asia, to that degree caste structures have correspondingly appeared in the societies that have ingested it. There is no such thing as "quasi-caste," as Dumont contends, in Ceylon and other regions peripheral to India. There is either "caste" or there is not "caste" and the degree of its presence depends on how deeply and in what form the Brahmanic system penetrated these peripheral regions and what 'use' was made of it by the cultures already in place there. These points are implicit in the topics covered in the second and third papers contained in this volume.

Thus, internal and comparative evidence tend to mutually reinforce our thesis that the caste system is not simply a type of social structure that is wholly confined within the ambit of pan-Indian civilization, narrowly conceived. Rather it is the transmuted outcome of the impact of an historically evolved religio-cultural structure on a more widely diffused genre of social organization—that which I call ascription-oriented occupational stratification. This specific conjuncture of social and cultural structure established itself as the foundation of Indian civilization, imparting a systemic unity and consistency to the social life of all societies and peoples of this region. Through trade, migration and messianism (both Hindu and Buddhist), selective aspects of this complex also impacted on the rest of Asia and, depending on the specific forms which contact assumed in different societies, gave rise to 'royal liturgies,' patterns of social stratification and other social phenomena on the Indian model. These exported manifestations of caste, to repeat, were not "quasi-castes" as Dumont contends but authentic versions of the systemic phenomenon itself arising in response to the same processes that gave rise to it in its native habitat. In Southeast Asia and Ceylon, the importance of royal courts as ritual structures was considerably greater than was the case in India, to be sure, but what is important is that they nevertheless replicated the Brahman-Kshatriya symbiosis and perpetuated the ideology of *varna* for the same reason this was done in India—*viz*, for resanctification and pollution-management. In eastern Asia (China, Tibet, Korea and Japan), untouchability had exactly the same implications as it had in the Indic world because it stemmed from the same karmaically-rooted and occupationally-centered preoccupation with pollution. In this sense, one could say that 'pan-India' did spread to and in varying degrees penetrate the cultures and consequently impacted on the social structures of the rest of Asia.

To understand how the caste system came into being in its original pan-Indian version one must understand what moral-philosophical developments transpired within this cultural milieu which, in effect, led to a convergence between religion and an occupationalized division of labor. In the papers which follow I put it that Hinduism occupationalized the religious order and sacralized the occupational order. This was accomplished over centuries by the evolution of what Weber (*Ibid*) called a 'theodicy' because it purports to explain why there is evil and death in the world and how this may be overcome. The innovators of this theodicy were the Brahmans and the success of their mission lay in the fact that the basic moral and cosmological concepts out of which it was constructed became universally diffused (varying only in nuance) through all of the sectarian varieties of Indian religious experience and penetrated all of the *cultures* that were dispersed over the Indian subcontinent. How this took place is suggested by the quotation which keynotes this chapter, by Srinivas's study of the Coorgs (*Ibid*), and by my paper in this volume (Chapter Four) comparing *jajmani* relationships in the Nilgiri Hills and on the northern Indian plains.

There can be no question that Hinduism arose in a cultural milieu that was coming to be dominated by what Schweitzer (1960) termed 'world and life renunciation' Trends in this direction seem to be suggested by ceramic seals and other archaeological data associated with the Indus Valley Civilization dating as far back as the third milennium BC.[21] But even if this degree of antiquity is not ultimately substantiated, the impulse to regard mortal existence as entrapment in organismic processes which must be overcome by the practice of austerities, mystical introspection and Vedic rituals under the guidance of spiritual mentors until life is transcended is clearly in evidence from the sixth or seventh centuries BC onward. We know that as Hinduism evolved in the gangetic plains and slowly diffused throughout India, permeating a wide range and variety of societies as it did so, it underwent an enormous institutional development and acquired a phenomenal philosophical, doctrinal and ritual corpus expressed through many sectarian systems. But as the proponents of a 'sociology of India' have amply shown, it is possible to identify a set of regularities which underly this multifarity of form and style. This is true for the basic concepts which gave social substance to the caste system. No matter how different the sectarian manifestations of Hinduism may appear to be on the surface, it becomes clear on close inspection that all of them proceed from certain fundamental assumptions and lead the believer toward certain basic conclusions. Moreover, the internalization of this body of assumptions and conclusions presupposes the existence of a social system with definite parameters. Caste was the most crucial of these parameters.

From a sociological standpoint, the most important passage in the R g Veda is paragraph 90 of Book X—the so-called Purusha myth.' Here we find stated in a most succinct manner the social structural foundations of the developing Brahman 'theory' of society. This is *varna*, the social framework within which a doctrine that will conceive of mortal life as an episode in an unimaginably long and complex quest for life-trasncendance can be carried out. It is also the initial announcement that the system of occupational stratification already present in the early state systems of the punjabi and gangetic plains is to be the model for structuring ritual interaction. Identifying the structure of society with the structure of nature and with the supernatural essence that encompasses all being, while simultaneously stressing the fact that everything is born and sustained through sacrificial ritual, the narrative declares: "With Purusha as offering, the Devas performed a sacrifice... On the grass they besprinkled him, the Sacrifice Purusha, the first born. With him the Devas sacrificed, and those Sadhyas and the Rishis....When they divided Purusha, how many portions did they make? What did they call his mouth? What his arms? And what his thighs and his feet? The Brahmana was his mouth, and his arms were made the Rajanya, his thighs became the Vaishya, and from his feet the Sudra was born." (p. 287).

This entire passage bespeaks of the permeation of the sentient world with divine essence through religious sacrifice. Society itself (*varna*) is sacralized and becomes an instrumentality of the sacrifice. "The Deity," in Bose's (*Ibid*) words, "allowed his absoluteness to be sacrificed so that he could be manifested in the world of space and time." (p. 287) This conceptualization of society also has organic and hierarchical implications which are important for the future but at this stage of Indian social history it is doubtful if these aspects of the social structure were conceived in any fundamental way differently from the way they were generally conceived in the early state systems. That is, society composed of hierarchically ranked yet functionally interdependent occupational strata.

The religio-cultural developments which build on these Vedic beginnings and consummate in the Hindu caste system occur in subsequent periods as the so-called Aryan and indigenous societies undergo synthesis.[22] The key milestone, according to Pandharipande (1986), is the Brahmanas, for out of this 'literature' came the *Purwa Mimamsa* ('earlier interpretation') which enunciated the doctrine of *karma* as it has been subsequently understood in Indian religion. *Karma* and *samsara* are the binary conceptualizations, the cultural inventions, if you will, which fully transform a system of ranked, stratified, ascriptive occupations, characteristically found in preindustrial civilizations, into the indispensible social structural vehicle through which salvation as life-transcendence must be sought.

This is clear when we factor into our analysis the entire body of basic philosophical and cosmological concepts which evolved from the period of the Vedas through the ensuing periods of the Brahmanas and the original Upanishads[23] and which became universalized across the entire spectrum of Indian society. Besides *varna*, *karma* and *samsara* were the concepts of *brahman*, *atman*, *moksha*, *dharma* and *maya*. Together these came to comprise a 'conceptual package' that is at the root of Indian civilization and whose actualization in behavioral terms both requires and facilitates that special or idiomatic adaptation of ascription-oriented occupational stratification which is called the caste system.

All Indic religious systems have as their ultimate purpose life-transcendence (*moksha*) because all assume that sentient existence is a false perception of reality (*maya*), the facade behind which lies The One (*tat ekam*), *brahman*, who, formless, and because formless eternal, is the sole reality. All that is perceived by the senses, all that we are attached to by virtue of our physical existence, is transitory (subject to death and decay) and therefore unreal (*maya*). The 'purpose' of existence is actually not to 'attain' identity with this ultimate being, as some interpreters claim, but to simply tear away all impediments standing in the way of discovering that what is true and permanent in individual being (*atman*) is already nothing more than ultimate being *brahman*.[24]

Thus, conscious, mortal existence entails immersion in life process. To the priestly minds that evolved this system of thought the biological realities of organismic existence seemed to somehow represent the opposite of what immortal existence and being must be. They saw the blood and gore associated with birth, the suffering and deformations associated with disease and violence, the repugnancies associated with waste effusions from the human body, and the decay and putrification associated with death as all connoting imprisonment in a body and a world which, as long as one could find no way to transcend it, must remain irretrievably entangled in it for life after life. Mortal existence was permeated with polluting substances whose control and systematic reduction through time, requiring Brahman-supervised rituals in one's present life and upward-spiraling rebirth (*samsara*) over the long pull, were the essential ingredients for finding a way out (*moksha*).

With *karma samsara* at its heart, this conceptual package, operating in the context of the pre-industrial state, makes the caste system entirely understandable. Caste in any of its specific manifestations, as the work of Dumont and Pocock prepared us to realize, is a social manifestation of ideological (i.e , cultural) structure internalized by the people of pan-India. The building-blocks of this structure, whatever its sectarian or denominational variations, were the basic moral-philosophical concepts already alluded to which Brahmanic thought evolved in the Vedas, the Brahmanas and the Upanishads.

The fundamental presupposition which makes the caste system necessary is that reality and immortality are one and the same thing and that this eternal state of being is by its very nature the opposite of everything that one associates with mortal existence. That which seems real through sensory perception is in fact unreal and that which seems unreal to mortals, because their senses and even their normal thought processes cannot perceive or imagine it, is the *only* reality. "Ignorance will not do!" proclaims the *Isa* Upanishad, "but knowledge is not enough!" Knowing is beyond knowledge :

11. The truth lies beyond,
    Beyond knowledge of knowledge and knowledge of ignorance;
    Ignorance leads to death, and
    Knowledge to after-death.
12. Plunged into dark darkness
    Are worshippers of Non-Being;
    Into greater darkness than those who
    Delight in Being.[25]

Transcendence can normally take place only by slow degrees because mortal existence in its entirety is arranged in one vast hierarchy which measures the degree to which any

THE SACRALIZATION OF A SOCIAL ORDER

living thing is immersed in life-process. The more immersed one is the more they are enshrouded in the karmaic residues which bar access to the Truth—*viz*, that all mortal existence is an illusion (*maya*) and *brahman* is the only reality. *Varna* is the social field within which humans are compelled to strive for life-transcendence. *Jatis* are the social compartments through which humans pass in each birth in the course of their karmaically determined quest for *moksha*, or release from life. *Varna* and *jati* are aspects of *maya* and reflect the fact that *dharma* (law) applies to everything that is contained within the cosmos. Even *maya*, the veil that conceals the Truth, is *structured illusion*, and all who are caught up in it are subject to the laws that govern it.

Karma is the action or behavior in which people engage during their lifetime within the ambit of their *jati*. *Dharma* ordains that certain occupational and ritual functions are appropriate behavior for persons in their given *jati*. The degree to which actual behavior conforms to these dharmaic specifications determines which direction on the status ladder the individual moves in their succeeding birth. *Samsara*, or rebirth, is concrete testimony as to the fidelity with which the individual has conformed to caste *dharma*—i.e., the moral significance of their actions.

How is the precise status-content of rebirth determined? The *Mimamsa* (4th century AD) provides the theoretical basis for answering this question. "This theory," declares Pandharipande, "has been used in Hinduism to explain why some people are born high (Brahman) or low (Sudra) caste."[26] Actions create 'tendencies' (*vasanas*), she continues, which get transferred to the next birth. This happens because the 'residues' of acts performed in this life (*sanciyamana*) leave 'traces' on *atman/jiva*, the particulate of *brahman* that is encapsulated within the physical body (*deha*). These are responsible for the creation of the *vasanas* which a person manifests in their next incarnation. And, it might be added, these tendencies are underlyingly *the reason why* the individual's *atman* remanifests itself in a *deha* socially encompassed by a particular *jati*. For that incarnation is a precise moral reflection of what the *karma* of previous birth warrants in that case.

The distinction between *atman/jiva* and *deha*, and their

interrelationship in the karmaic chain, also helps us to understand why the dichotomy between pure and impure, emphasized in the work of Dumézil and adapted by Dumont and Pocock, is such a crucial factor in the Hindu 'theodicy.' Pandharipande points out that only the body (*deha*) is subjected to *karma*. *Atman/jiva* is pure essence (*brahman*), immune to the pollution and death that attends immersion in life-process. Conscious action, or 'free will,' in Hinduism entails striving to attain that state of being (*moksha*) in which (*karma*) is overcome and pure being is conjoined. It is this which identifies *varna/jati* as coterminously sacrificial and social structure in Hocart's terms. Karma renders *every* human action ultimately ritual in nature for every action has bearing on how deeply the *deha* in which *atman/jiva* is imprisoned is compelled to be immersed in the pollution of life-process. Rituals of sanctification, if correctly performed, are karmaic acts which avert deeper immersion than one's present *jati* already implies and facilitate rebirth into a higher *jati* that moves *atman* closer to consummating its identity with that pure essence (*brahman*) which exists beyond *maya*, beyond pollution.

Occupations (*jati*) are functional attributes of a sacralized stratified social order (*varna*) in which mortal actions (*karma*) simultaneously facilitate the conduct of orderly economic (*artha*) and secular (*kama*) life and the pursuit of salvation (*moksha*). Releasing *atman/jiva* from the bonds of *maya* is the end-product of social interaction. *Jatis* are divinely fixed, ritually differentiated status reference points. Social mobility consists of *atman/jiva*, garbed in *deha*, passing through these dharmaically determined social compartments by successive rebirths (*samsara*) in its trek towards salvation.

The ideological structure which delineates the social field within which this process takes place can be literally 'conjugated' by simply applying the principle of 'opposition' or 'reciprocal repulsion' (terms employed by Dumont and Pocock following Demézil and Bouglé) between pure and impure to the hierarchy of interdependent functional specializations recognized by the Purusha myth. The most encompassing of these oppositions is between the Once Born and Twice Born, between that is, those whose functions (*karma*) entail such a high degree of defilement that Brahmans cannot minister to them and those whose order of defilement is not so great as to bar the priestly ministrations of Brahmans. The sacred thread ceremony (*Upanayana*) ritually distinguishes between these two subdivisions of Hindu social space. Within the domain of the Twice Born are further oppositions from which Brahmans (priestly functions), Kshatriya (political and military functions) and Vaishyas (mercantile, agricultural, pastoral and artisan functions) are derived. One is the opposition, or perhaps symbiotic interdependence would be a more apt term, between Brahman and Kshatriya. This arises from the need for royal power to be continuously resanctified by priestly (i.e., ritual) power in order for the former to retain its sacred legitimacy. We noted this fact earlier in our comparison of the relationship between priest and king in India and Ceylon. "It is not enough," says Dumont (1962), "that the king should employ Brahmans for the public ritual, he must also have a permanent, personal relationship with one particular Brahman, his *purohita*. . ." (p. 51) This is crucial because:

> The gods do not eat the offerings of a king devoid of a *purohita*. . . so that the *purohita* presides, as *hotr* or *brahman* priest, i.e., as sacrifator or controller, to royal sacrifices. Moreover, the king depends on him for all actions of his life, for those would not succeed without him. (p. 51)

The second opposition is between Brahman-Kshatriya, on the one hand, and 'the other' Twice Borns (i.e. Vaishya), on the other. It is the distinction between the interlinked possessors of supernatural and secular power and those whose occupations are 'clean' but are not formally implicated in the system of power. These latter may also receive the ministrations of the Brahmans, of course.

Within the domain of the Once Born there is the single *varna* which designates meniality and association with polluting functions. But this is subdifferentiated between Touchable and Untouchable Sudras. It recognizes the fact that some occupations, while 'unclean' (i.e., cotton weaving, iron smithy, carpentry etc.) are not ultimately polluted while others (animal scavenging, barbering, clothes-washing) are. The latter constitute those functions that are directly involved in pollution-removal and absorbtion which I have called 'contra-priestly' (see Chapter Four) because their performance is as essential to Hindu society as are those performed by Brahman priests.

The four *varnas* stand for empirical society structured to facilitate the operation of the Hindu value system. As by-products of the Purusha myth, they assign religious significance to occupationally conceptualized social functions (priest, king, merchant, artisan, farmer, menial) in such a way as to provide a basis for classifying and ranking hundreds of individual specializations (*jatis*) comprising the division of labor. The *varna* scheme, put another way, was the ethnosociological instrumentality by which ascription-oriented occupational stratification was 'pan-Indianized' in South Asia. It is this classificatory structure which facilitated the assimilation into Hindu society, as civilization grew and expanded over the centuries, of 'outside' communities by enabling them to become transmuted into *jatis* which were assignable to a *varna* in accordance with the moral implications and politico-economic potency of whatever occupationalized functions with which they became primarily identified. Conquering (i.e., politically powerful) tribes or communities, for example, whether of indigenous or exogenous origins, tended to become 'kshatriyaized' over time. Pastoral tribes tended to become 'vaishyaized' (e.g., *gawalas* in the gangetic plain) in the same fashion.

Varna provided the ideologically legitimized moral matrix within which the ritual requirements of the Hindu belief system could be elaborated in social terms. The sacralized division of labor provided a permanent inventory of occupational specialists who could simultaneously keep the economy running and provide the various ritual specialists needed to keep the religious order intact. Brahmans and Untouchables (priests and contrapriests) were perpetually available in their hereditary social compartments to perform the ritual tasks that sustained the delicate balance between purity and pollution upon which the quest for salvation depended. Against the gauge of *varna*, the *karmaic* implications of each *jati* could be accurately assayed. The progress of *atman/jiva* through the successive rebirths of the *dehas* encapsulating it could be measured. And most of all, the moment of salvation, life-transcendence, could be foreseen.

As the ensuing essays are read, it is hoped that this introductory discussion will constantly be borne in mind. For though the essays are 'dated' in the sense that they were written at various times and for various purposes over the years, all address in their own way the range of issues alluded to here. In the author's view, each essay adheres to the basic theses adumbrated in this chapter. Together they add up to a coherent sociological picture of a social institution which we shall probably never fully comprehend and which, in any event, may soon be changed so radically by the steady march of modernity that its traditional lineaments will no longer be recognizable anywhere in contemporary India.

REFERENCES

[1] This quotation is taken from the authors' discussion of M. N. Srinivas's *Religion and Society Among the Coorgs of South India* by Dumont and Pocock (1965, p. 42) undertaken in *Contributions to Indian Sociology*, No. 3. The statement is made in the course of disputing his interpretation of the meaning of certain Coorg rituals. While Srinivas contended that the rituals and ritual objects connoted their pre-Hindu roots as an originally separate cultural community that was subsequently 'Hinduized,' Dumont and Pocock held that nothing could be gained from this analytical approach because in fact the Coorgs had already become "one particular kind of Hindu" as was true with all other identifiably "Hindu groups." My purpose in selecting this passage for a keynote statement is to emphasize my concurrence with the thesis that Hindu society, and its dominant social structural feature, the caste system, arose wherever a basic set of Hindu values diffused and were 'internalized' by a local population which had heretofore not possessed this value configuration, and most importantly acted socially in terms of it.

[2] This was an introductory essay to an edited volume whose authors explored the nature of caste in South India, the Hindu and Buddhist regions of Celyon, and Muslim north Pakistan. It was a 'comparative' perspective on caste, to be sure, but only within the greater South Asian region. This perspective impressed Leach with "the special qualities of intercaste relationships" so much so that he felt impelled to conclude that :

There is something fundamentally wrong about Kroeber's well-known definition. 'A caste may be defined as an endogamous and hereditary subdivision of an ethnic unit occupying a position of superior or inferior rank or social esteem in comparison with other subdivisions' (Kroeber 1931). It is wrong because it puts the emphasis in the wrong place—upon endogamy and rank, and that every caste in a caste system has its special privileges. (p. 10)

[3] References to the relevant archaeological data are contained in the text and footnotes of these articles in particular.

[4] Gerald D. Berreman (1960) opened this debate in The American social science community at the commencement of the sixties with his seminal and provocative paper published by the *American Journal of Sociology*, entitled, "Caste in India and the United States."

[5] Most important, of course, were the nine consecutive annual issues of *Contributions to Indian Sociology* (1957-66) which they edited and through which they promulgated their social anthropological viewpoint on the caste system.

[6] Marriott and Inden, in a number of provocative studies, have carried the 'inside view' of caste to ultimate levels. In their 'ethnosociological' approach, the authors relate the structure of caste interaction to what they believe to be an indigenously Indian conception of the relationship between substance and morality. "Bodily substance and codes for conduct are...thought not to be fixed," they declared in 1972, "but highly malleable, and not separated but mutually imminent features: coded substance moves and changes as one thing throughout the life of each person and group." (p. 4) In this way they appear to move the study of caste out of the domain of comparative sociology altogether and consign it to the comparative study of epistemological foundations of the relationship between the nature of matter and moral philosophies. "At the first glance of a Euro-American, South Asians appear to possess the same sort of dual categories," Marriott and Inden assert. However, upon deeper reflection, "It has long been disturbingly evident in many small ways to Westerners...that South Asians do not insist on drawing a line between what Westerners call 'natural' and 'moral' things..." Consequently, "By redefining old data in indigenous cognitive terms, we have tried to understand caste systems freshly as part of what South Asian thought sees as a changing and variegated, but rather consistently structured flow of coded natural substance." (p. 17)

[7] See F. G. Bailey's (1959) rejoinder to the Dumont and Pocock thesis, entitled, "For a Sociology of India?"

[8] Berreman contributed two chapters to the volume edited by De Vos and Wagatsuma (1967) entitled, "Structure and Function of Caste Systems," (Chapter 14) and, "Concomitants of Caste Organization," (chapter 15) in which he further elaborated his comparativist perspective on caste. Schermerhorn (1972) offered a critique of Berreman's work on caste from his vantage as a professional sociologist which pointed to what he saw as some of the conceptual pitfalls of (ironically) insufficiently taking account of culture in differentiating caste systems. Schermerhorn is disturbed by what he calls "Berreman's cavalier dismissal of a religious foundation for the phenomenon of caste." So eager is he, declares Schermerhorn, "to repudiate this that he allows himself to make inordinate claims that are implicitly contradicted by other authors in

THE SACRALIZATION OF A SOCIAL ORDER 23

the same (De Vos and Wagatsuma) volume." (p. 257) This criticism, however, does not detract from the importance of Berreman's critique of narrowly culturalogical approaches to the study of caste.

9Passin's (1955) was probably the first recognition of a partial connection between untouchability in eastern Asia and the diffusion of Buddhism.

10The volume edited by De Vos and Wagatsuma (1967) was the first, and so far the only attempt to make systematic comparisons of the sociological and psychological characteristics of untouchability and related caste phenomena outside pan-India.

11Klass (1980) addresses himself to the orig'ns of caste in South Asia employing a methodology which he claims is "ec'ectic." Dismissing every prior attempt that has been made to explain the emergence of the caste system, Klass opts for a demograph'c-ecological explanation. Assuming that there was already pressure for agricultural land prior to the Christian era when the caste system formed, (a highly dubious assumption, it might be said), he hypothesized that this generated powerful pressures on the landed to share their harvest surpluses with a 'surplus' landless population. Caste groups somehow are supposed to have formed out of this 'imbalance' by a process of occupational subdifferentiation of various non-cultivating tasks associated with the agricultural economy and the economic maintenance of agricultural communities. There is a vague allusion to the existence of 'the value system' as having something to do with determining how different occupationalized tasks were allocated in accordance with their desirability. This highly speculative 'theory' must be listed in the comparativist category as an extreme manifestation thereof which totally dismisses the relevance of Hinduism to the origins and development of at least the foundations of the caste system. It will be seen in the essays in this volume that I cannot accept its validity.

12It is my primary hope that the reader will see that my approach to the study of the caste system does not hold that a choice need be made between the two intellectual positions. Cultural and social structural analysis both have their place in a complete interpretation of the caste system.

13"For a thousand years," says Woodcock (1966), from the sixth century BC to the fifth century AD, there were Greeks in India." He continues:

> They traveled as explorers in the pay of the Persians and marched as soldiers in Alexaaner's army, they came as wandering philosophers and seaborne traders, as artists and ambassadors, as administrators and princes. They founded kingdoms and cit'es, and the list of Greek kings and queens who reigned in India and on its borders is as long as the list of English kings and queens who have reigned in England since the Norman Conquest. There were few parts of India into which the Greeks did not eventually penetrate. (p. 13)

See also Dahlquist, *Megasthencs and Indian Religion* (1962).

⁴⁴See, for example, Samuel Beal, *Travels of Hiouen-Thsang* (4 vols., 1957-58); Wheeler and Macmillan, *European Travellers in India* (1956); Kaul, *Travellers' India: An Anthology* (1979).

¹⁵The literature which this class of observer produced is voluminous. Examples of its scope can be gained by examining the "Tribes and Castes of India" volumes such as William Crooke's *The Tribes and Castes of the North-West of India* (4 vols., 1974), or studies of the agrarian system, such as Baden-Powell's *Land Systems of British India* (3 vols., 1972).

¹⁶Nadel's full statement (p. 82) reads: "...any class of relationships is more completely removed from 'actual happenings' than is any class of action, so that the order of phenomena to which relationships belong —the order of grouping or Society—represents an abstraction of a higher order than the order of action or Culture." Thus, 'interstratum relationships' characteristic of ascription-oriented occupational stratification systems (priests, kings, merchants, farmers, etc.) are more abstract than are inter-stratum relationships between Brahmans, Kshatriyas, Vaishyas and Sudras in Pan-India. The latter set of interrelationships are only one cross-cutting set of such interstratum relationships confined to a single, circumscribed territory or region and do not exhaust the total number of action systems (or Cultures, in Nadel's terms) which together provide the basis for identifying the genre of social organization (in this case, ascription-oriented occupational stratification) to which it belongs.

¹⁷Mainly under topical rubrics such as 'village studies,' 'kinship', 'pure and impure', 'tribe and caste,' 'kingship,' etc.

¹⁸For a good review of this literature and analysis of the contemporary contexts and meanings of the caste system, see Pauline Kolenda (1978).

¹⁹Von Furer-Haimendorf (1951) believes there is evidence among the tribal cultures of eastern India to suggest the existence of eschatological beliefs which presage (since the tribal cultures pre-date the rise of Hinduism) both *samsara* and *karma*. Regarding afterlife:

> Here we find a clearly developed concept of the soul of the psyche type, separable from the body even during this life. It is this soul which finally enters the Land of the Dead, there to lead a life closely resembling life on this earth and then to die again and move to the next Land of the Dead. Such a belief in a sequence of nether worlds may have played an important part in developing the idea of the transmigration of souls...(p. 48)

And regarding *karma*:

> some of the hill-tribes of Assam and Burma, such as the Lushais, believe that success in war, in the chase, and in amatory adventures, as well as the expenditure of wealth at elaborate feasts of merit, will secure to a man a privileged fate in the Land of the Dead, and it may be that the quest for such merit which outlasts death foreshadows the idea of *karma*. (p. 48)

THE SACRALIZATION OF A SOCIAL ORDER 25

Robert Hertz (1960) drew similar conclusions in his essays *Death and The Right Hand*. He found all through the Southeast Asian cultures beliefs concerning the ritual condition of corpses and the afterlife which appear to reflect a logic not dissimilar to that which impelled Hinduism to adopt the practice of cremation and the concepts of *karma* and *samsara*.

[20]Among many studies of social stratification in Southeast Asian societies, see Mabbett (1977) and Rabibhadana (1975). These studies and an unpublished paper by Van Esterik (1975) suggest that caste (in this case *varna*) ideology diffused into the region but did not result in caste structures on the Indian model. Speaking of Thailand, Van Esterik holds that "a caste system was never developed independently in Thailand" because: "under conditions of low population density, interdependence between hill and plains social systems, and the need to exchange widespread resources such as minerals, a system of individual differences in status positions linked by negotiated patron-client relations is much more compatible with prehistoric, historic and ethnographic evidence." (p. 16) Mabbett notes that in Angkor there are many inscriptional references to *varnas*. However:

> .. all such references to royal power over *varnas* are intended to convey that particular rulers controlled their subjects, and frequently also that these rulers had literary graces; but they are valueless as historical evidence that *varnas* were in any sense like their Indian equivalents, or that they were in reality social classes *created* and maintained by kings. (p. 433)...it seems more appealing to regard *varnas* as privileged orders or dignities to which favored individuals were appointed by the king. (p. 435)

'Caste' took the form of honorific and sacerdotal statuses in the royal court instead of as an organizational rubric applied to the division of labor writ large. It was a question of adapting the organizational principles and sacerdotal presuppositions inherent in *varna* to an indigenous social structure (in this case the royal court) which seems to have found it an attractive means of achieving cultural enhancement.

[21]For the most up-to-date information on the archaeology of the Indus Valley Civilization, see Possehl (1979, 1982).

[22]Humayun Kabir provides a helpful discussion of synthesizing processes in Indian civilization in his book, *The Indian Heritage* (nd).

[23]One of the best compilations of the original Upanishads in the English language remains *The Thirteen Principal Upanishads Translated from the Sanskrit* by Robert Ernest Hume (1951), first published in England in 1951. About these treatises, Hume says:

> The older Upanishads are religious and philosophical treatises, forming part of the early Vedas. The preceding portions are the Mantras, or Hymns to the Vedic gods, and the Brahmanas, or directories on and explanations of the sacrificial ritual...the Upanishads, being integral parts of the Brahmanas, are continuations of the sacrificial rules and discussions, but they pass over into philosophical considerations. Much that is in the Upanishads, particularly in the Brihad-Aranyaka

and the Chandogya, might be more properly included in the Brahmana portion, and some that is in the Brahmanas is Upanishadic in character. *The two groups are closely interwoven.* (p. 5. Emphasis is mine.)

[24]This, of course, is the import of the famous Sanskrit declaration: *ahm Brahm asmi tat tvam asi* ("*I am Brahman, that thou art*"!)

[25]This translation was prepared by P. Lal.

[26]The paper, authored by Professor Rajeshwari Pandharipande, from which this quotation was taken, entitled, "Free Will: A Hindu Perspective," was presented at the Seventh Annual Inter-Religious Dialogue, The Margaret Gest Program of Haverford College, April 5, 1986. I am deeply indebted to Dr. Pandharipande for very helpful discussions concerning caste as explicated in the traditional textual materials and many insightful suggestions as to how these can be reconciled with a modern sociological interpretation of caste. I am also grateful for her willingness to undertake a critical reading of the manuscript before it went to press.

BIBLIOGRAPHY

Baden-Powell, B.H., *Land Systems of British India*, New York: Johnson Reprint Corp., 4 vols., 1972 (originally published in 1892).

Bailey, F. G., "For a Sociology of India?", *Contributions to Indian Sociology*, No. III: 88-101, July 1959.

Beal, Samuel, *Travels of Hiouen Thsang*, Calcutta. Susil Gupta, 4 vols, 1957-58.

Berreman, Gerald D., "Caste in India and the United States,' *American Journal of Sociology*, Vol. 66: 120-27, 1960.

——————' "Structure and Function of Caste Systems" (Chapter 14), and "Concomitants of Caste Organization" (Chapter 15), in De Vos, George and Hiroshi Wagatsuma, *Japan's Invisible Race: Caste in Culture and Personality*, Berkeley: University of California Press, 1967.

Bose, Abinash Chandra, *Hymns from the Vedas*, New York: Asia Publishing House, 1966.

Bouglé, Celestin, *On the Caste System*, Cambridge University Press, 1971.

Crooke, William, *The Tribes and Castes of the North-Western India*, Delhi: Cosmo Publications, 3 vols., 1974 (originally published in 1896).

Dahlquist, Allen, *Megasthenes and Indian Religion*, Stockholm: Almquist and Wiksell, 1962.

De Vos, George and Hiroshi Wagatsuma, eds, *Japan's Invisible Race: Caste in Culture and Personality*, Berkeley: University of California Press, 1967.

Dumont, Louis, *Homo Hierarchicus*, University of California Press, 1970,
Dumont, Louis and David Pocock, *Contributions to Indian Sociology*, No's I, II, III, IV, V, VI, VII, VIII, IX, The Hague: Mouton, (annually), 1957-1966.
von Fürer-Haimendorf, Christoph, "The After-Life in Indian Tribal Belief," The Frazer Lecture in Social Anthropology, 1951, *Journal of the Royal Anthropological Society of Great Britain and Ireland*, Vol. 83, Part 1: 37-49, January-June, 1953.
Hertz, Robert, *Death and the Right Hand*, London: Cohen and West, 1960.
Hocart, A. M., *Caste: A Comparative Study*, London: Methuen, 1950.
Hume, Robert Ernest, *The Thirteen Principal-Upanishads Translated from the Sanskrit*, Oxford University Press (revised second edition), reprinted, 1951.
Inden, Ronald, "Exchange, Sacrifice and Hierarchy in Early India," unpublished paper, University of Chicago, May, 1969.
Kabir, Humayun, *The Indian Heritage*, New York: Harper and Brothers, nd.
Kaul, H. H., *Travellers' India: An Anthology*, Delhi: Oxford University Press, 1979.
Klass, Morton, *Caste: The Emergence of the South Asian Social System*, Philadelphia: Institute for the Study of Human Issues, 1980.
Kolenda, Pauline, *Caste in Contemporary India: Beyond Organic Solidarity* Menlo Park, Cal.: Benjamin/Cummings, 1978.
Leach, Edmund, ed., Aspects of Caste in South India. Ceylon and North-West Pakistan, Cambridge University Press: 1-10, 1960.
Mabbett, I. W., "*Varnas* in Angkor and the Indian Caste System," "*Journal of Asian Studies*, XXXVI, No. 3: 429-442, May, 1977.
Marriott, McKim, "Hindu Transactions: Diversity Without Dualism," prepared for the Symposium, "Transactional Analysis," *Association of Social Anthropologists*, Oxford University, July 9, 1973 (revised version July, 1974).
Marriott, McKim and Ronald Inden, "An Ethnosociology of South Asian Caste Systems," presented at the Symposium, "New Approaches to Caste and Kinship," annual meetings of the *American Anthropological Association*, Toronto, December 1, 1972.
————,' "Caste Systems," article prepared for the *Encyclopedia Britannica*, March 26, 1973.
Nadel. S. F., *The Foundations of Social Anthropology*, Glencoe, III.: The Free Press, 1951.
Pandharipande, Rasjeshwari, "Free Will: A Hindu Perspective," presented at The Seventh Annual Inter-Religious Dialogue, The Margaret Gest Program of Haverford College, April 15, 1976.
Passin, Herbert, "Untouchability in the Far East," *Monumenta Nipponica*, Vol. 2, No. 3: 27-47, 1955.
Possehl, Gregory L., ed., *Ancient Cities of the Indus*, New Delhi: Vikas, 1982.

————————,' *Harappan Civilization*, New Delhi: Oxford Publications, 1982.

Rabibhadana, Akin, "Clientship and Class Structure in the Early Bangkok Period," in G. William Skinner and A. Thomas Kirsch, *Change and Persistence in Thai Society: Essays in Honor of Lauriston Sharp*, Ithaca: Cornell University Press, 1975.

Schermerhorn. R. A., "A Note on the Comparative View of Caste," *"Phylon*, Vol. 33, No. 3; 254-259, 1972.

Schweitzer, Albert, *Indian Thought and Its Development*, Bombay: Wilco, 1960.

Srinivas, M. N., *Religion and Society Among the Coorgs of South India*, New York: Asia Publishing House (second printing), 1965.

Van Esterik, Penny, "Caste and Caste Ideology in Southeast Asia," unpublished paper, University of Illinois, 1975.

Weber, Max, *The Religion of India: The Sociology of Hinduism and Buddhism*, Glencoe, Ill.: The Free Press, 1958.

Wheeler, James Talboys and Michael Macmillan, *European Travellers in India*, Calcutta: Susil Gupta, 1956.

Woodcock, George, *The Greeks in India*, London: Faber and Faber, 1966.

2

Caste and Class:
A Comparative View

Until fairly recently the study of social stratification was largely the province of sociology. Anthropology had less to offer on the subject because traditionally it had concentrated its attention on the small-scale, simpler societies where elaborate systems of social stratification were by definition nonexistent. If anthropologists had anything to say about stratification processes it was mainly with reference to social ranking of the type found in nomadic communities, on Pacific islands, and among sedentary peoples whose numbers were modest and whose technological base permitted a limited division of labor. Sahlins has pointed out that "Status inequalities in primitive societies are not accompanied by entrepreneurial enterprise and the complete separation of producers from the factors of production" (1958, p. 2). "Social classes" is a term that should be applied to "the social strata of market-dominated societies." he says, while "categories of rank in kin societies" should be termed "status levels" (p. 3). Sahlins concludes: "Modern sociological definitions of class which stress occupational standing, class antagonisms, differences of interest, and the like are not applicable to societies of the primitive order,' (p. 2).

The situation changed after W. Lloyd Warner (1949) put anthropological field methods to work studying the social class system of Yankee City and V. Gordon Childe (1942, 1951) began using archaeology to trace the evolutionary emergence of complex technological systems and their social structural concomitants. Henceforth anthropology entered ever more deeply into the study of largescale modern and modernizing societies. The cross-cultural comparative and holistic frame-works of the discipline richly complemented the techniques of systematic sampling and institutional analysis that sociologists had developed to investigate Western societies. Anthropology enabled students of social stratification to achieve a broader perspective on this phenomenon, from the standpoint of both time and space. The Western experience with the functional and evaluative classification of work could be contrasted with that in Africa, Asia, Polynesia, and elsewhere and all such classificatory systems could be viewed in evolutionary terms.

This discussion will reflect the growing collaboration between sociology, anthropology, and the other social science disciplines pertaining to one of the most fundamental of all questions asked about social stratification in large-scale human societies—namely, what is the difference between caste and class. Our focus will be on a comparison between Indian and Western society, the two culture areas in which the distinctions between these social categories have been the most sharply drawn. The goal will be to see if it is possible to identify some of the fundamental principles and processes that determine the nature of caste and class, the relationships obtaining between them, and the transformations they undergo in the face of social and technological change.

I

The notion of caste evokes a picture of fixed statuses and occupations, of social immobility firmly solidified by rules of endogamy. The country that has always seemed to epitomize this state of affairs is India. But this view of India is not an exclusively modern perception; the Greek adventurers and scholars who followed in the wake of Alexander the Great shared it. After the great Macedonian conqueror burst into India through the Kabul River valley, these men brought home to Europe accounts of a system of irrevocably assigned occupations that differed little in fundamental characteristics from those the European explorers and merchants brought back seventeen centuries later. The latter accounts do not differ much in spirit, though perhaps considerably in detail, from modern sociological descriptions of this phenomenon.[1]

The geographer Strabo, writing in the first century B.C. but drawing on materials compiled during Alexander's campaigns and by historians attached to the court of Seleucus Nicator,[2] speaks of seven castes: philosophers, cultivators, herders, traders and laborers, fighting men, inspectors, and administrators. Although these castes are different in composition and order from the classical Hindu *varnas*, a member of one caste is nevertheless "not permitted to contract marriage" with a person of another caste "or to change from one profession or trade to another" (Jackson, 1907, pp. 39-40). Today we would say that Strabo had confused *varna* and *jati* (see below under "Caste in India").

In 650 A.D., the Chinese Buddhist scholar-pilgrim Hsuan Tsang traveled through India and recorded his impressions of the people and cultures he encountered. Said he:

> The people of India are divided into castes: the Brahmans are noted particularly on account of their piety and nobility. Tradition has so hallowed this class that there is no question as to the difference of place, but the people generally speak of India as the country of the Brahmans ....(Jackson 1907, pp. 124-125)

Regarding the other castes:

> The second is called Kshatriya, the royal caste. For ages they have been the ruling class: they apply themselves to benevolence and mercy. The third is called Vaisyas, the merchant class; they engage in commercial transactions and seek for profit at home and abroad. The fourth is called Sudra, the agricultural class; they engage in cultivating the soil and occupy themselves with sowing and reaping. These four castes form different classes of ceremonial purity. The members of a caste marry within their own class....(Jackson, 1907, p. 125)

The picture of Indian social organization presented almost exactly one millennuim later by a Dutch missionary, Abraham

Roger (1640), differs in no fundamental respects from Hsuan Tsang's. From a Brahman informant he learned that there are:

> ...four general castes or races in this nation. For though it seemeth that five castes should be reckoned there to, yet they (the Brahmans) say there are four, since the fifth is not truly counted among the castes [i.e., its members are "untouchables"]. These four are the caste of Brahmines, the caste of Settreas, of the Weinjas [Vaishyas], and of the Soudras. They follow each other in order, like as they are placed here, and also surpass each other in honor. So that the first and most esteemed is the caste of Brahmines. (Jackson, 1907, p. 238)

A visitor to India today still finds a caste system fitting the foregoing descriptions. Describing a caste as "a social unit in itself" Hutton declares:

> The customs by which it lives are generally different in some respects from those of other castes, and are sometimes in marked contrast to those of any other caste at all. Persons of one caste do not marry those of another. The extent to which persons of one caste will eat or drink with those of another is strictly limited by unwritten laws and everybody knows who is affected by them. (Hutton, 1963, p. 2)

What is different about India today, of course, is that this ancient pattern of social organization has competition; it must share the social stage with a different system of social organization tied to an emerging techno-economic order radically different in its premises from those of the system that made caste possible. The student of social stratification is thus in a position in contemporary India to concern himself not simply with caste in the classical sense but with what is happening to castes as they and the social order to which they are wedded undergo modifications in the face of industrialization and the considerably more open society accompanying it. The task for the student of social stratification on a worldwide comparative basis is to ascertain what the transformations and modifications of caste structure in India tell us about processes of social segmentation and classification of human populations in large-scale societies generally.

II

Many scholars have inclined toward the view that the caste system of India is a unique phenomenon with no true counterparts elsewhere. If they are correct, of course, it is idle to attempt to fit caste into any sociological context concerned with separating general processes of social stratification systems arising out of their integration into local and regional culture complexes. Caste becomes at most what Edmund Leach has conceived it to be—a social structure confined to the Pan-Indian cultural world. "I do not accept the view," he says, "that, because caste is a structural phenomenon, it is therefore a concept which has worldwide application." On the contrary, it "denotes a particular species of structural organization indissolubly linked with what Dumont rightly insists is a Pan-Indian civilization" (Leach, 1960, p. 5) Hutton concurs in this view:

> ....caste in its fullest sense, that is, as we know it in India, is an exclusively Indian phenomenon. No comparable institution to be seen elsewhere has anything like the complexity, elaboration and rigidity of caste in India....It is virtually inconceivable that the association of circumstances necessary to produce so complex an institution...could ever be found in more than one area of the earth's surface (Hutton, 1963, pp. 40-47)

Although scholars of Leach's and Hutton's persuasion are right in insisting that India's caste system is, in its ethnographic manifestation, a unique sociocultural phenomenon, they are wrong in implying that for this reason the system has come about by processes that are fundamentally different from the way in which systems of social stratification have come into existence at other points in time elsewhere in the world. Their error arises from a failure to make better use of social history, an insufficient appreciation of the conceptual tools that empirical archaeology has made available for studying the evolution of social organization, and a tendency to ignore the principle of saliency in data selection. When such factors are taken into consideration, India can be as readily employed as any society as a point of departure for discussing general processes of social stratification.

To be sure, Indian civilization and the Hindu religion are phenomena too complex to have occurred as such more than once in human history. But so is the specific concatenation of factors that have led to *any* individual civilization in human history! Both archaeology and social history teach us that most of the basic structural properties associated with the state system within which Hinduism arose were by no means unique. State organization commenced in India after 2800 B.C. in the Indus Valley (see Wheeler, 1966). The fundamental ingredients of the civilization had diffused into the subcontinent from the Middle East where they originated (Wheeler, 1966, Childe, 1942, 1951, and Piggott 1950 offer discussions of this). Whatever uniqueness may be found in the Indian way of life was erected upon this foundation. What we are actually dealing with in the case of India, therefore, is a single type of a social species which has been variously called the "premodern complex society," "traditional society," "urban civilization,," "preindustrial civilization," etc. This species can be viewed as a highly complex ecological system which evolved about six thousand years ago. Its main characteristics were technical command over agricultural, masonry, ceramic, metallurgical, and other major productive processes, the systematic harnessing of fire, animals, and water as energy sources, the integration of large populations into patterns of work through occupational specialization, and the refinement of social mobilization and control through the development of state and ecclesastical organizations.

The sociological view of this human achievement was first systematically expounded by V. Gordon Childe (1942, 1951). Although he was Marxist in ideological commitment, and although the inherent nature of archaeological data tends to breed a materialist bias, Childe's theory of social evolution was not simply a case of naive technological reductionism. The dawning of civilization in the Fertile Crescent was to him a result of the simultaneous and interdependent evolution of technology and social structure. This can be made clear by examining a key passage in *Man Makes Himself*.

> And so by 3000 B.C. the archaeologist's picture of Egypt, Mesopotamia, and the Indus Valley no longer focuses attention on communities of simple farmers, but on *states embracing various professions and classes*. The foreground is occupied by priests, princes, scribes and officials, and an army of specialized craftsmen, professional soldiers, and miscellaneous laborers, all withdrawn from the primary task of food production. The most striking objects now unearthed are no longer the tools of agriculture and the chase and other products of domestic industry, but temple furniture, weapons, wheelmade pots, jewelry and other manufactures turned out on a large scale by skilled artisans. As monuments we have instead of huts and farmhouses, monumental tombs, temples, palaces and workshops. And in them we find all manner of exotic substances, not as rarities, but regularly imported and used in everyday life. (Childe 1951, pp. 115-116; emphasis mine)

Childe is depicting the rise of state systems in the Old World out of a Neolithic base that had steadily undergone amplification over the six preceding millennia. There is now an enormously complicated division of labor, with an economic system oriented toward markets and international commerce; cultural life is integrated around a rudimentary concept of nationality; and the material and social resources of society are being marshalled and exploited by elites. Demographic, technological, sociological, and cultural scale have all markedly increased and combined to form a new ecological structure for man—the state which manages the lives of countless individuals more efficiently than small hunting and agricultural communities managed the lives of a few.

One sociological implication of the developments described by Childe is that, for the first time in human history, work had become *occupational*. Specific skills became a recognized, formalized basis for socially demarcating the members of society, rewarding them differentially, and treating them differently. Functional differentiation is, of course, a fundamental property of all social systems and it is not this as such that represents a new departure in social evolution at this time. Paleolithic hunters and Neolithic agricultural communities[2] divided up the work according to age and sex differences as do simple societies today. What was different was, first of all the *scale* of the functional differentiation involved, as already noted, and even more the *form* it now took. Instead of assigning functions according to age, sex, and other biological criteria, a whole range of functions were increasingly assigned to categories of individuals according to their avowed capacity to perform them, their ability to co-opt them, or their inability to avoid being compelled to perform them. Occupational categories became a fundamental structural component of human social life in state systems. These categories cut across, subsumed, and articulated with older categories of social differentiation. Often occupational groups, such as merchants, formed communities in their own right whose social networks extended beyond the frontiers of individual state systems. Most important, the conception of work as occupational was not confined to the production of material goods but was extended to embrace a variety of "nonmaterial" functions that were deemed essential to the operation, maintenance, and extension of state systems. Childe speaks of scribes, priests, princes, soldiers, and officials—occupations just as specialized and formalized as carpenters, potters and blacksmiths. Thus, at one level, a state system could be conceived as a network of interdependent occupational roles which facilitated both the production of economic goods and services and cultural and social integration of the state system itself.

The invention of such a vastly complex "ecological machine" as this demanded mechanisms that not only successfully managed large numbers of individuals but that sociologically managed large numbers of different occupations. Occupational recruitment and classification now became major problems in their own right. Since societies are in essence bundles of differentiated roles that are both functionally interdependent and evaluatively ranked, how does one cope with literally hundreds of different occupational roles? What social organizations are needed to achieve a measure of functional integration among them and assign them their relative social worth? Clearly hundreds of formally differentiated occupational roles could not be individually ranked. This exceeded even the classificatory skills of man! Just as clearly, the functions of individual occupational roles had to be viewed and judged according to their place in larger social structures whose overall functions made major contributions to the operation of the state system writ large.

The development of systems of social stratification as aspects of the development of the state systems themselves was man's response to these problems. Orderly, integrated systems of managing large numbers of occupational roles and larger numbers of human beings were attained through the classificatory device of grouping or categorizing them. Put more simply, some occupations had so much in common that making discriminations of rank among them was neither necessary nor feasible. Carpenters, potters, weavers, and glassblowers all had in common the facts that they were artisans and that each received about the same remuneration for his work. Determining "worth" and therefore "rank" by monetary means, in fact, became a major evaluative instrument because the market became the dominant mechanism for regulating the flow of goods and services in the state systems and the primary basis for determining the worth of the product that a role occupant produced.

A further differentiation between power and degree and type of control over economic resources was implicit in the very process of monetizing markets and occupationalizing work. Eric Wolf has expressed this very well:

> In the course of cultural evolution... simple [productive] systems have been superseded by others in which control of the means of production, including the disposition of human labor, passes from the hands of primary producers into the hands of groups that do not carry on the productive process themselves, but assume instead special executive and administrative functions; backed by the use of force. The constitution of such a society in such a case is no longer based on the equivalent and direct exchanges of goods and services between one group and another; rather goods and services are just furnished to a center and only later redirected. (Wolf, 1966, p. 13)

Thus the vertical differentiation of occupational roles—that is, the ranking of them—reflects distinctions between control over the producers and the producers themselves. It further reflects the difference between producers whose products are commodities requiring high levels of skill and producers whose only real product is the sweat of their brow. A fundamental distinction among elites, skilled artisans and technicians, and menials was created at the inception of state systems. Elites were those whose control of resources and producers gave them political power over society itself. Artisans and technicians had the power to mold resources into objects and products highly valued by society. This made them indispensable to elites as well as other consumers and gave them favorable access to the material and symbolic rewards which state systems could dispense. Menials lacked both power over resources and the skills needed to mold them into indispensable objects. This condemned them to subservience to both the elites and the artisans.

We can say, therefore, that the social stratification systems that became associated with the preindustrial civilization always sorted occupational roles into a minimum of three strata reflecting a subtle admixture of power and functions. I would call these simply, (1) power-elite roles, (2) technical implementation roles and (3) menial roles. We can see this process of vertical categorization, or stratum-ranking, at work in the *Rig Veda*. In a passage that may date from before 1000 B.C., we encounter the following:

> When they divided Purusa, how many portions did they make?
> What do they call his mouth, his arms? What do they call his thighs and feet?
> The Brahman was his mouth, of both his arms was the Rajanya made.
> His thighs became the Vaisya, from his feet the Sudra was produced.
>
> (Renou, 1963, p. 45)

This Vedic hymn mentions four strata rather than three but it is clear that these early Hindu thinkers contemplated a subdivision of the elite into a priestly (Brahman) component and a secular political (Rajanya—what was later called Kshatriya) component. Vaisya[3] represents the congeries of occupations located by analogy in that part of the body where the vital functions are performed, sustaining, as it were, the arms and the head as well as the feet. And Sudra, of course, embraces the occupations concerned with primary production—the growing of food, manual labor, and so on. These are the unskilled and menial occupational roles that are assigned to the socially powerless and that free the elite and artisan occupation groups to concentrate on skills completely divorced from the quest for day-to-day subsistence. This "caste system," then, is actually a classic exemplification of the hierarchy of social stratification which Childe elucidated for the old Bronze Age civilizations.

To understand further the nature of social stratification in the preindustrial state systems, we must turn to the problem of role recruitment, or "role allocation," depending on one's vantage point. For it is here that in many respects the crucial distinctions between the occupational role systems and concomitant social stratification of the early civilizations and those of the present are to be made. I do not overlook fundamental differences in technological order when I say this, as will be made clear by the time this discussion has been fully developed, but I am for the moment concentrating attention on social structures alone.

Nadel has said, "I view roles as modes of acting 'allocated to individuals' by the norms of the society..." (1957, p. 35). Professor Linton (1964) long ago distinguished two basic ways in which individuals take on the various roles they play as members of society. One he called "ascription" and the other "achievement," by which he meant simply that either you "inherit" a status and concomitant bundle of behaviors associated with it or you "acquire" them by more direct and personal initiatives. In the former case, such as with a kinship role, learning the appropriate behavior is just as essential to its effective operation as it is in the case of an acquired or achieved role. What is different is that the ascribed role is "reserved" for the individual and internalizing the behavior appropriate to it is regarded as mandatory. This mandatory quality is absent in the case of the achieved role, or at least it is not in the forefront of the formula prescribed for acquiring its attributes.

In the simplest terms, I think we can say that ascribed roles are those that are identified by social norms as inherited in the same way as somatic traits. As Nadel puts it, " the governing property is an inevitable or fortuitous state in which individuals find themselves...as when mature age carries with it such-and-such privileges (or responsibilities)." With achieved roles, "the governing property is a behavioral attribute, active or passive, which individuals are free to choose as a goal or objective" (Nadel, 1957, p. 36).

In preindustrial state systems work was made occupational but occupations were primarily ascribed. Put differently, occupational role and role occupant were regarded as being identical. This is what sets the occupational sociology of preindustrial state systems apart typologically from that of the industrial societies that were to come later. And it is precisely in this domain of role recruitment that the relationship between the occupational role system and the technological system is most dramatically visible.

Childe and other sociological archaeologists regularly referred to preindustrial state systems as "urban societies" because the type of community that seemed more than anything else to typify what they had become was the city. There full-time nonagricultural specialists of all kinds abounded and exchanged their wares for the food produced by the peasants in the hinterlands. There were born and flourished the intellectual, political, and administrative arts whose applications to human affairs gave state systems both cultural meaning and empirical substance. But from the standpoint of understanding the occupational sociology of the old civilizations it is important to realize that (a) ancient cities were comparatively small in size and (b) the proportion of a state's population living in them ranged from only four or five percent to a maximum of twenty percent. This meant that technology could actually sustain a very limited number of nonagricultural specialists. Most members of these societies continued to live in agricultural villages where they specialized in food production and in certain other occupations (carpentry, blacksmithing, pottery) that supported the activities of farmers. Life in all three types of communities among which populations were distributed—cities, towns, and villages—remained essentially on a modest level of complexity where in the majority of cases social identities could be determined by knowledge of one's forebears. The production of goods and services did not occur in factories but in families or other group settings that were modeled on kinship principles. Guilds were one type of unit for the recruitment and integration of specialized producers in urban contexts which transcended conventional kinship organization. Yet, according to Gideon Sjoberg in his book *The Preindustrial City*,

> ...among the qualifications for [guild] membership, kinship ranks paramount. We have already mentioned the primacy of kinship ties in numerous spheres of activity in the preindustrial city. It is the ideal and usual pattern for a son to follow in the footsteps of his father...(Sjoberg, 1963, p. 19)

The face-to-face quality of interpersonal interaction, especially in the context of individual communities, combined with a technology which required that work be made occupational but which could not facilitate removal of occupations from the control of domestic groups and kinship systems, accounts for the ascriptive nature of most occupations and the comparative rigidity of social stratification. Men inherited their occupations from their fathers because occupations were regarded as another piece of property equivalent to all other objects, statuses, and obligations that were transmitted from one generation to the next. Whether in Egypt, Babylon, Persia, or India, the belief that occupational role and role occupant were identical pervaded society and was thought to reflect the nature of the cosmos itself. To be sure, occupational mobility occurred regardless of this, and its degree varied in accordance with historical and culturally idiosyncratic factors, but it was rarely encouraged *in principle*, which is, after all, the crucial issue here. This distinction will become clearer when we turn to the substantive case of India. For now let us simply emphasize the point that all occupational stratification systems associated with preindustrial states were essentially castelike and that India merely constituted one manifestation of this general type. In this sense it was not a unique social phenomenon as Leach, Hutton, and Dumont imagined.

Before turning to the Indian caste system, however, it is necessary to direct attention to one other important feature of the ascriptive occupational role system found in preindustrial state systems. This is what I would call its uniquely accommodative quality. The old state systems arose gradually out of ethnic diversity as well as technological variety. Prehistoric and protohistoric man, at the threshold of civilzation, consisted of numerous bands of Paleolithic hunters, possibly some nomads, and Neolithic farmers whose communities dotted the river valleys from Egypt to the Indies. Each such band or community (or at least clusters of each) had a separate collective identity, based on a separate culture, including distinctive nuances of technological style, its own language or dialect, and its own system of social organization. These communities and bands were, in essence, separate societies, ethnically distinct, on a lower level of social and technological evolution than state systems.

The state systems were an interesting compromise between the need for a higher level of social integration to facilitate the effective exploitation of new technology and the impulse for separate survival of the ethnically diverse populations that became enmeshed in their market economies and political hegemonies. The latter were able to survive and retain a recognizable identity to a remarkable degree because work could be occupationalized without being removed from the control of ascriptive social units such as family, band, tribe, or village. Such units, or sections of such units, could move *en masse*, as it were, under the structural rubric of state systems and keep their internal cultures and social organization fairly intact so long as they provided some specialized product or service to the larger economy and polity. In an ascriptively oriented occupational system it makes little difference whether the supplier of a specialized service or product inherits his skills and status from his father or from his mother's brother. The Persian empire presumably manifested a high level of skill and sophistication in accommodating an enormous variety of ethnically distinct peoples into an efficient economy and harmonious polity (John Howland Rowe refers to this in his article on the Renaissance foundations of anthropology, 1965).

If we may borrow an idea and some terminology from

Lèvi-Strauss's remarkable essay "The Bear and the Barber" (1963), it could be asserted that societies with ascriptive systems of occupational stratification employed kinship structures to produce closure so that they could be *exopractical* respecting some function or complex of functions that contributed to the operation and integration of the social system of which they were components. In the case of the Fertile Crescent cultures the "functions" were occupations relevant to economic, political, administrative, and religious spheres of experience. Since closure and consequent functional interrelationship were the aims, units could be strictly occupationally specialized aggregations (like guilds and certain castes) or they could be whole tribes, parts of tribes, migrant Asiatic nomads, etc. These could have matrilineal, patrilineal, or bilateral descent systems. They could practice polygamy or monogamy. All that was important in the last analysis was that whatever form their internal social organization might take, they had to ensure that a specified occupation be performed by members who internalized their occupational role as part of their general system of descent.

This dimension of occupational integration in the pre-industrial state systems goes a long way toward explaining the extensive cultural pluralism frequently observed to be a characteristic of them and, of course, provides a basis for dealing with the Indian caste system as something more than an isolated anachronism unrelated to broader processes of social evolution.

III

In calling attention to the occupationalization of work in the emergent state systems of the ancient Middle East, we by no means exhaust the forms that social stratification has taken in human history. There have always been and still are culture areas where factors other than occupations have constituted the central pivot of social stratification. Sub-Saharan Africa, for example, underwent a basically independent pattern of social and technological development which produced results considerably different from those in the Fertile Crescent and the other Eurasiatic river valleys. There social stratification seems to have been the outgrowth of what Nadel (1954) has called the "conquest state." In the societies of this region ethnic, political, and military considerations, more than technological elaboration, provided the central criteria for the hierarchical ranking of persons and assignment of differential functions to them. Discussing the conquest of the Nupe kingdom of Northern Nigeria by the Muslim Fulani, Nadel notes that the Fulani "raised the Holy War of Islam against the Pagan kingdoms and their rulers" and successfully established themselves as a ruling dynasty. This "hereditary aristocracy bears special titles and formerly claimed important legal and ceremonial prerogatives" (Nadel, 1954, p. 6). Beneath them were arrayed other strata whose ranks were determined by their military and administrative functions and only incidentally by birth. Thus:

> The Fulani government of Nupe, then, represents a clear case of social stratification which arose in consequence of conquest and *pari passu* with the foundation of a conquest state. The social stratification is partly one of caste—if by caste we mean the rigid and unalterable apportionment of social privileges on the grounds of descent. Partly the stratification is only one of class, based on differentiation in political and economic power which is not rigid, but permits of movement between the strata, in accordance with capability, with services rendered—especially in war—with success and luck; that is, it permits "social mobility." (Nadel, 1954, p. 6)

The Nuba clans also represent a kind of social stratification that is based neither on conquest nor on "occupations' in the strict sense of the word." Instead, they are differentiated in terms of what Nadel calls "mystic duties." He continues:

> There is no differentiation in ordinary occupations, all being farmers and owners of livestock. But there is an important differentiation in ritual rights and obligations. For each clan is believed to possess certain supernatural powers peculiar to it and to no other clan, which enable it to control a part of the universe...... Not only for its own

benefit but...on behalf of the tribe at large, so that together, the clans ensure—in a supernatural sense—the survival of the tribe and safeguard its welfare. (Nadel, 1954, pp. 14-15)

Two clans even qualify as "untouchables," it would seem, inasmuch as their "mystic duties" cause them to be avoided out of fear of what the misdirection of their supernatural powers might lead to.

The American South constitutes still another case where occupational specialization has not been the dominant factor in the way that it was in the Old World in producing a highly ascriptive system of social stratification. But this comparison cannot be developed until we take a more detailed look at caste in India.

IV

From what I have said about the sociology of occupations in preindustrial state systems of the Middle East, it is clear that I regard the caste system of India as a particular manifestation of ascriptive occupational stratification.

Both archaeological evidence and internal evidence from early Hindu texts suggest that the caste system gradually crystallized within a succession of state systems not basically different in technology and social structure from their progenitors in the Fertile Crescent. The first high civilization in India was the so-called Indus Valley or Harappan Civilization, which consisted of two major cities, Harappa and Mohenjo-daro, and a vast hinterland punctuated with towns and peasant villages. This state system came into existence around 2850 B.C. and endured for approximately fifteen centuries. There seems little doubt that its inspiration emanated from the locus of Old World civilization to the West. Says Sir Mortimer Wheeler:

> Intellectually the founders of [the Indus] civilization had one crowning advantage. Two great riverine civilizations had shortly preceded them, in Mesopotamia and Egypt... The Indus Civilization, with its individual technology and script and its alien personality, was no mere colony of the

West. But ideas have wings, and in the third millennium the *idea* of civilization was in the *air* of western Asia. (Wheeler, 1966, pp. 61-62).

At this early stage, the occupationalization of work was clearly in evidence. The cities, towns, and villages reveal all the usual signs that men were categorized by the kind of work they did and ranked according to the social value assigned to their work. Citadels containing large public buildings indicate the existence of a state political and administrative apparatus capable of managing large-scale populations and indeed *requiring* the services of a full range of occupational specialists.

Large public baths in the citadels of Mohenjodaro and Harappa plus terracotta seals depicting Brahma bulls, cobras, shiva-like deities, etc., suggest a Hindu religious development as yet insufficiently elaborate to transform the ascriptive occupational order into true caste. As Pusalker says:

> No buildings have so far been discovered...which may be definitely regarded as temples, and even those doubtfully classed as such have yielded no religious relics. There are no shrines, altars, or any definite cult objects...All we have to rely on for reconstructing the religion of the people is the testimony of the seals, sealings, figurines, stone images, etc. (Pusalker, 1957, pp. 195-196)

The transition to the caste system occurred when Hinduism matured into an institutionalized religion and began transforming the social organization of Indian state systems to accord with its metaphysical, philosophical, theological, and ritual presuppositions. This was the achievement of the Brahman priesthood. By sociological processes that are still far from understood, because they are so inadequately documented, this priesthood evolved into a stratum of religious specialists situated at the apex of Indian society and empowered to set the standards of religious belief, moral conduct, and occupational rank for virtually the entire subcontinent.

The Brahman caste and the social stratification system its members fashioned came into existence as and to the degree that they succeeded (a) in applying a body of concepts about the religious implications of occupationalized work to the ascriptively stratified state systems in India and (b) in projecting the concept of occupational differentiation into the domain of religious experience. In short, the Brahmans invented and propagated a religion that sacralized the occupational order and occupationalized the sacred order. Brahmanism (the religion of a sacerdotal priesthood) was the point of departure for the Pan-Indian civilization of which Leach and Dumont speak. The caste system was the social structural embodiment of Brahmanic values.

What do I mean by the conclusion that the Brahmans sacralized the occupational order and occupationalized the sacred order ?

One of the most important metaphysical pre-suppositions underlying the development of Hinduism was *maya*. This has been translated as the "doctrine of cosmic illusion" but it is doubtful if this phrase really conveys the concept's full implications. To understand the concept fully one needs to realize that behind *maya* lies an organismic model of the cosmos that emphasizes some rather surprising features of biological processes. In the Purusa vivisection referred to earlier we saw that social differentiation was conceptualized on the analogy of a human organism. Not only is society arranged in a hierarchy of functionally specific segments, but these segments are, like the organs of a body, mutually interdependent. The feet, although low in rank, are no less critical to the whole being than the head or the arms.

But the model goes a step beyond this rather simple and obvious structural analog. It was believed that involvement in the phenomenal world meant attachment to life (biological process) and attachment to life meant, in turn, entrapment in the web of decay, death, and rebirth associated with life. This vicious cycle would continue endlessly unless one learned the secret of transcending phenomenal existence (*maya*). That secret was embodied in the single sentence, "I am Brahman, that thou art." It meant this: he who realizes that the essence in man, his soul (*atman*), is identical with the essence that underlies the cosmos (*brahman*) will cut his ties to the phenomenal world and enter a state of eternal bliss (*moksha*). Accomplishing this required the progressive termination of one's immersion in life processes, which in social terms meant gradually rising through the caste system until final enlightenment facilitated the annihilation of transitory existence altogether. Each *varra*, or social stratum, represented a degree of immersion in life process. Within the *varna* an individual was a member of an occupational category (*jati*) that was considered hereditary (role occupant=occupational role). It was assigned to that *varna* because it was one of a number of occupational categories all of which were thought to represent about the same degree of immersion in life process. Each occupational category was essential to the functioning of the whole society; for this reason the moral code ordained that the path to salvation lay in conforming to the *dharma* or "laws governing conduct" for that *jati*. By performing the functions (*karma*) ordained by the dharma of one's caste, rebirth into a higher category was assured, and each higher category represented less immersion in life process and correspondingly increased comprehension of what the true end of existence was —namely, *moksha*.

Other perceptions of biological process, in addition to organic integration, that were incorporated into the Brahmanic metaphysical model account even more for the remarkable uniqueness of both caste and ritual behavior in India. The perception that organisms, when alive, produce a variety of wastes and excrescences and, when dead, decay made a profound impression on the early sages (see Orenstein's interesting discussion of the basic premises of Hinduism, 1968). More than anything else this perception seems to have stood for the implications of attachment to and immersion in the phenomenal world. The conclusion was drawn that in both the occupational and religious domains of experience the degree of immersion in life could be gauged by the extent to which a person's activities put him in proximity to blood, death, and dirt. Contact with the offal and decay of life was impure and defiling and unequivocally opposed to those attributes of being that survived after mortal existence had been transcended.

In mortal existence, therefore, status was determined by degree of immersion in life process. In the context of religious conduct, this meant that rituals were oriented toward making things "clean," toward coping with the defilement that pervaded the phenomenal world. In the context of occupational conduct, this meant that the rank of any given profession was determined by the relationship that obtained between its practitioners and defiling things.

Occupation and ritual met and reinforced each other because of the special kind of pollution problem that existed in the Brahmanic Hindu world. Avoiding and overcoming pollution were both dealt with in interactional terms. Contact between occupational categories had to be so structured that there could simultaneously be efficient economic exchange of commodities produced and efficient social circumscription of physical contact between the producers, the latter because of the differentially polluting implications of the kinds of work they did. Contact in religious ceremonies had to be structured on the model of the division of labor for the same reasons. For a ceremony to be valid, two classes of ritual specialists had to participate. One was the Brahman priest who, himself meticulously groomed for his religious role, dispensed to his client the benefits of his own state of superior purity. That state of purity was ultimately derived from the fact that his profession removed and insulated him from all forms of work and other mundane activities that defile. As long as the Brahman scrupulously adhered to his caste *dharma* he embodied the highest state of religious purity attainable by corporeal man and could, as it were, transmit this purity to members of his client's household by performing rituals for them. He was paid for his services in return. The other class of specialists was what I call the defiled "contra-priests" (see Chapter IV). These were the *jatis* in the Sudra stratum at the bottom of Hindu society who practiced such defiling occupations as washing clothes, barbering, sweeping, removing dead animals, midwifery, and cremating the dead. As it were, they absorbed the defilement inherent in dealing with blood, death and dirt so that the rest of Hindu society could be free of it and partake of the rituals that prepared the ground for rebirth into ever purer occupational categories, culminating in mystical union with *Brahman*. The Hindu Jajmani system, so widely studied by social scientists and economists (Wiser, 1936; Kolenda, 1963; Gould, 1964), is nothing more than the economic expression of the kind of social stratification and interaction that the

Brahmanic Hindu conceptualization of the nature and sources of pollution necessitates. A *jajman* is anyone who receives the services of priestly purity—dispensers and contra-priestly pollution removers. Both of the latter are called *pujan* and must be distinguished from each other in terms of the "vantage" they respectively represent on the pollution-removal problem.

A. M. Hocart attributes the origins of caste to particular styles of kingship which arose in the state systems of South Asia. "The conclusion we have arrived at on modern evidence," he says, "is that the caste system is a sacrificial organization, that the aristocracy are feudal lords [sic] constantly involved in rites for which they require vassals or serfs, because some of these services involve pollution from which the lord must remain free" (Hocart, 1950, p. 17). Dumont and Pocock go further in identifying what is specifically Indian in the attempt to control defilement. It is "the employment of specialists who take upon themselves a part of the impurity, and to whom it remains permanently attached" (Dumont and Pocock, 1959, p. 18). The general characteristic of asserting an identity between occupational role and role occupant in preindustrial state systems was intensified by sacralizing the ascriptive occupational order and occupationally differentiating the sacred order. Contra-priests, "by virtue of their specialized ritual functions, live permanently in that state of impurity which they help others to abandon as rapidly as possible" (Dumont and Pocock, 1959, p. 18).

Thus, what made the caste system "Pan-Indian" was not its ascriptive quality *per se*. Ascriptive stratification was typical of all the preindustrial civilizations in the Eurasiatic river valleys. Its distinctiveness arose from the fact that Hinduism integrated the occupationalization of work and the stratification of occupations into a metaphysical model that made no hard and fast distinctions between economic and religious functions. All occupations were "moral statements," so to speak, and key behavioral components of rituals were "stated" in occupational terms. The result was a tremendous proliferation of occupational categories, or *jatis*, based on an almost limitless variety of functional criteria. Because the degree of social closure imposed upon *jatis* by pollution concepts was so extreme, they attained an order of internal cohesion and ethnic self-consciousness approximating that encountered in tribes and other culturally separate communities. While this facilitated the integration of formerly separate tribal communities into the fabric of Hindu society, it also placed definite limits on social homogeneity. India became the most elaborately stratified preindustrial state system in history.

V

We can now address ourselves to the question raised earlier about possible similarities between racism in the southern United States and Hindu caste. Harper (1968) and Berreman (1960, 66) have made some interesting and useful comments on this matter, as has Dumont (1965). Harper has said, for example, that "One of the obvious ways in which the two countries differ is in the number of units comprising the caste society." Whereas the number found in the Hindu caste system runs into the hundreds, in America there are only two. In a similar vein, Berreman has declared:

> It would seem that occupational specialization—functional complementarity—is characteristic of most caste systems. Whether or not this is a usual defining characteristic and whether or not it will exclude some societies heretofore described as caste societies remains to be seen. It depends partly on how rigidly one applies the definition. Is the southern Negro, for example, an occupational specialist? (Berreman, 1960, p. 300).

From my theoretical standpoint, one observes that both the Hindu and Southern systems are ascriptive in nature; both tend to fuse the individual to certain specified, culturally important roles through the mechanism of descent. The roles so demarcated are not all expressed in simple economic terms. There are powerful tendencies to "moralize" the functional differences recognized and apply some of them to behavioral systems not connected with the market. Both premodern India and the *antebellum* South were highly rural societies where statuses were comparatively easy to assign and enforce. Beyond this point, however, similarities are harder to discern because the cultural premises underlying the two caste systems were radically different in many fundamental respects.

We have seen that caste differentiation and hierarchy in India were extremely complicated. They came about through the sacralization of an already well-developed ascriptive occupational order, and by application of a model for functional differentiation derived from this to the domain of ritual activities. An organismic world view and emphasis on pollution removal as the desideratum for attaining salvation united all categories of specialists, regardless of their rank, into a symbiotically interrelated whole. Although dominance and subordination were integral parts of intercaste behavior, and disgruntlement and at times open hostility against the privileged by the deprived members of the system always existed, what was nevertheless striking about Hindu society was the uniformity with which certain values permeated all layers and categories of the society. With all their felt deprivations and hostility to the status quo, Hindu Untouchables saw themselves to a remarkable degree as part of the system, as subcribers to the *meanings* underlying it. This has been made clear by contemporary studies of the phenomenon called "sanskritization" (see Srinivas, 1962), in which low castes endeavor to raise themselves not by rebelling against the caste system but by adopting the symbols, rituals, and social pretensions of the pure castes.

The Southern social system produced two hierarchically arranged strata, as already noted. Historically these had their roots in a division of labor between master (the owner of the means of cotton production) and slave (the compulsory supplier of labor for cotton production). This economic order was the point of departure for the eventual development of a "racial caste system" much as the ascriptive division of labor originating in the Fertile Crescent was the substructure upon which the Hindu caste system was erected. The system itself embodied a configuration of values that evolved in the South as a defensive reaction against the anti-slavery movement which culminated in the Civil War and the Reconstruction Era. Put differently, an intensification at the national level of the equalitarian-individualistic philosophy, which was a legacy of the Renaissance and the Enlightenment, generated an intensification of a regional counter-philosophy in the South. While summarizing Myrdal (1942), Dumont observes:

> The period 1830-1860 sees the development of an ideology for the defense of slavery: slavery being condemned in the name of natural equality, its champions argue against this doctrine of the inequality of the races; later the argument is used to justify discrimination, which becomes established from the moment when, about 1877, the North gives up [trying to enforce] assimilation, (Dumont, 1961, p. 40)

What began as an essentially economically motivated undertaking—the importation of African slaves and their integration into the plantation system as cheap labor—later became an institution primarily oriented toward the production of social inferiority. Religious values did not predispose Southern society toward an acceptance of organically harmonious sets of functionally differentiated social compartments. Rather, an impinging equalitarianism drove the Southern aristocracy and bourgeoisie to reformulate the central moral-religious values of Western civilization into a "sick" rationalization for the perpetuation of an inherently unfair (from a Judeo-Christian standpoint) social order. So-called Jim Crow was the culmination of this process.

Caste in the Southern United States was considerably more rigid than it was in India. Vertical movement was always possible on a limited basis in India by arranging marriages across *jati* boundaries. Berreman finds such "instances as these...an embarrassment to any definition of caste which makes endogamy requisite" (1966, p. 7). He observes, however, that "all these instances share with endogamy the fact that they comprise unambiguous rules for assigning a child its lifelong affiliation with a ranked group on the basis of its birth." The important point is that the ranked groups in the South were seen as racially distinct and therefore totally mutually exclusive, whereas in India they were seen only as occupationally and ritually heterogeneous and therefore not necessarily totally mutually exclusive in biological terms. To return to Lévi-Strauss's terminology: in India, endopracticality respecting marriages sustained groups whose chief exopractical functions were the production of goods, services, and/or ritually important activities. This system of mutually interdependent occupational functions was religiously sanctified *as a whole* so that all component units, regardless of status, were regarded as being equally engaged in the quest for salvation. Racial endogamy was politically imposed in the South, in contravention of America's dominant value system, by threats, terror, and murder. Its purpose was to compel blacks to perform the "function" of "producing" racial inferiority. Intermarriage was not possible because it would erase the biological boundaries upon which the whites' conceptualization of their superiority was predicated. Intermarriage could be permitted in India so long as occupational and ritual specialization were not disrupted, which is to say so long as the offspring of marriages could be jurally assigned to one or the other of the two status groups involved. Hypergamy and hypogamy, in fact, actually performed the positive function of adjusting discrepancies between ascribed and achieved statuses that might otherwise lead to serious attacks on the caste system.

VI

The Industrial Revolution in the West created a new set of technological premises for occupational differentiation, recruitment to occupational roles, and occupational stratification. A true social class system was born as the social concomitant of the birth of factories and the universalization of urbanization.

We usually mean two things by the term social class. First, to paraphrase our earlier definition attributed to Nadel (see page 40 above), "governing properties" of the roles associated with a class system are "behavioral attributes which individuals are free to choose as goals or objectives." Second, and following naturally from the first, ranking of the strata comprising such a system is preponderantly in accordance with economic criteria. This being the case, it may legitimately be asked whether such systems of social layering were really absent from human history until well into the eighteenth century in Western Europe. Did not China have a merit-oriented administrative bureaucracy dating back to the Han dynasty long before the beginning of the

Christian era (for a good sociological study of traditional Chinese bureaucracy, see Chang, 1955)? Was not the role of shaman in Central Asian nomadic societies and New World aboriginal societies a priestly status achieved by the most complicated and arduous processes of self-transformation (see Eliade, 1964)? Was not even the role of warrior-king associated with the status of Kshatriya in the Hindu caste system frequently attained by military success and political skill and then subsequently ratified or legitimized in Hindu terms?

The answer to all these questions, of course, is "yes." But they miss a fundamental distinction that must be drawn if we are to understand the respects in which modern technology was the basis for a genuinely new evolutionary departure in human social organization.

Throughout human history all cultures have designated a certain proportion of social roles as "achievable" because merit has seemed the best way to get the right person in the right job at the right time. But until the invention of steam (and later internal combustion) engines and their application to the driving of productive machinery, there existed no technology requiring the massive transformation of economic roles into merit-oriented statuses. Industrialization brought rapid economic growth and with it factories, the destruction of handicraft industries, the "depeasantization" of the rural segment of society, rapid and massive urbanization, and tremendous population increases. Sociologically, industrialization brought about the transfer of specialized occupations of all kinds from the context of kin groups to factories organized on bureaucratic principles. This meant that henceforth, and increasingly, occupational role and role occupant would be *in principle* separated; that the preponderant criteria for determining occupations would be "performance qualities"; and that economic rewards and social mobility would constitute the principal standards for evaluating the worth or status of any given role. What the industrial revolution brought about, then, to put it slightly differently, was a comprehensive social class *system* oriented to vast and complex markets, rooted in machine technology, and politically integrated by state systems immensely modified in structure. Previously there had been elements of social class in many different kinds of human societies, but *a true class system as the dominant feature of social organization in large-scale state systems* was a new phenomenon.

What all these changes boiled down to, in the last analysis, was more "open" societies. Such societies were still another ecological invention, which in this instance placed a premium on the scientific exploitation of the natural environment for human comfort and gain. Exploitation of natural resources was almost completely bureaucratized; and social organization was reconstituted to support the exploitative process. Separation of occupational role from role occupant was the sociological innovation that facilitated the massive bureaucratization of work. It established a direct and immediate relationship among performance, reward, and social mobility. And in the face of phenomenally expanding economies this literally altered man's entire perspective on the nature of society and human life. Philosophical and social movements like *laissez-faire* capitalism, the Enlightenment, and Marxism were direct manifestations of the efforts being made in industrializing state systems to understand, define, and legitimize the new technological revolution and its sociological concomitants.

Industrialization and the bureaucratization of work were contagious. This ecological process, which commenced in the English Midlands toward the end of the eighteenth century, had reached around the world and implicated in one way or another most of humanity by the middle of the nineteenth century. Both colonization and colonialism were by-products of the industrial revolution. Rapidly expanding European populations spilled out into the world and transplanted this ecological system to North America, Australia, New Zealand, and South Africa. The ravenous appetite for markets and natural resources associated with the system generated an explosive political expansion of the industrial societies until most of the rest of the world had been made the involuntary producers of raw materials for European factories and inveterate consumers of their finished products. Either you were a citizen of an industrial state system or you were the property of one.

Wherever industrialization spread, it radically altered basic premises of social life. Lipset and Bendix state as a "tentative interpretation" that "the social mobility of societies becomes relatively high once their industrialization, and hence their economic expansion, reaches a certain level" (1959, p. 13). To be sure, cultural variability may influence the transition from ascriptive to achievement-oriented systems of occupational recruitment and social stratification, but in the long run:

> Roughly comparable rates of mobility have been found under so many different social and economic conditions and in so many otherwise divergent samples that it may be more plausible to believe that the cause of mobility lies primarily in the economic expansion made possible by a given level of industrialization...(Lipset and Bendix, 1959, pp. 37-38)

The inexorability of industrialization and concomitant modernization processes, once set in motion, even in the case of colonially subjugated peoples, was foreseen clearly by Marx as early as the middle of the nineteenth century. Writing about India in 1853, Marx said:

> Modern industry, resulting from the railway system, will dissolve the hereditary division of labor, upon which rest the Indian castes, those decisive impediments to Indian progress and...power. All the English bourgeoisie may be forced to do will neither emancipate nor materially mend the social condition of the masses. , .[this] depend ng not only on the development of the productive powers, but [on] their appropriation by the people. But what they will not fail to do is lay down the material promises for both... (Marx, 1951, p. 67)

Indian nationalism began shortly after Marx wrote these famous lines, and was brought to fruition in 1947 by Gandhi and Nehru. The goal of the nationalists was to create a modern, independent India, free of ascriptive occupational roles and stratification structures. The nationalists themselves were, by and large, the most modern-oriented men in their society, who had gotten their education, as well as the ideas and techniques they wished to apply in India, from their British masters. Mr. Nehru repeatedly emphasized the need for "social justice" for the Indian people, which he described to his parliament in 1954 in this way:

> Our economy and social structure have out-lived their day and it has become a matter of urgent necessity for us to refashion them so that they may promote the happiness of all our people in things material and spiritual. *We have to aim deliberately at a social philosophy which seeks fundamental transformation of this structure...we must aim at a classless society* [i.e., at a merit-oriented occupational order] based on cooperative effort, with opportunities for all... (Nehru, 1954, p. 103; underlining and bracketed remarks mine)

India provides an interesting contemporary case of the birth of this new ecological system quite literally out of the corpus of its predecessor. We can observe what has happened to the caste system in the aftermath of British colonialism and judge whether industrialization has really "dissolved the hereditary division of labor," as Marx predicted.

Strictly speaking, of course, the Indian case is not entirely analogous to that of the Western nations. Imperialism limited the scope of technological change in subject countries like India for more than a century by limiting development to those sectors of the economy that served the needs of England's home industries. Sheffield was not interested in promoting the construction of steel plants in the colonies to compete with her own; she wanted mines opened to provide her factories with iron and tin ores, and unencumbered markets where the finished product could be sold at a profit. Manchester wanted the manufacture of cloth protected in the same manner. Thus, as Marx had observed, raw materials industries, railway systems, and public administration underwent the most spectacular development in India while the creation of the great industrial structures that alone afford the basis for completing an industrial revolution lagged far behind.

The result was a partial modernization of the Indian economy and social structure whose fulfillment could not be contemplated until a showdown occurred between the colonial administration and a mobilized nationalist elite. But the changes that even partial modernization brought were considerable, not only in the sense that they led to the political means for gaining Indian freedom but also in the sense that class-oriented values made formidable inroads in many parts of the society. Cities like Calcutta, Madras, Delhi, and Bombay grew into great metropolitan centers where opportunities for new occupations with statuses abounded. Modern education spread rapidly among the privileged castes and even made some progress among the masses. Enough industry got started to create the nucleus of an industrial labor force and modern administrative and managerial classes.[4] Mass consciousness of potentialities for social mobility, inherent in the new social order that was struggling to be born, set off a stampede of castes trying to improve the economic lot of their members and win official recognition of claims to higher status that had been assigned them in the traditional hierarchy. (Studies by the Rudolphs, 1967, Srinivas, 1962, 1966, and Hardgrave, 1969, provide excellent insights into these processes.) Death rates declined with scientific public health policies and the population began the steady climb associated with the commencement of industrialization (see Kingsley Davis, 1951).

With independence in 1947, there followed a series of "five-year plans" that generated capital inputs for all forms of modern economic and social development. Basic industries were promoted on a major scale for the first time in Indian history, and the effect of this soon became apparent in the social organization as well as in the economy and technology of the country. The result appears to be no different in basic terms from the results wrought by similar levels of input at comparable stages in the West's modernization. Between 1951 and 1951, the total work force increased 35 percent from 139.5 million to 188.4 million. The agricultural work force increased 34 percent (from 36.5 to 52.2 million). Workers in manufacturing increased even more rapidly from 12.5 to 20 million, or by 60 percent. Between 1901 and 1961, India's population grew 84 percent from 238.4 million to 439.2 million, and the trend toward urbanization during this period was evident. Whereas the rural population grew 69.5 percent (from 212.6 to 360.3 million), the urban population grew by almost 206 percent (from 25.8 million to 78.9 million). The source of the figures in this paragraph is the *Census of India*, 1961.)

However, despite all these changes, more than 80 percent of India's people were still living in peasant villages in 1961. Because the birth rate did not decline substantially, there were very high absolute increases in population. Unspectacular rates of economic growth continued to plague efforts to complete the processes of industrialization and social reform. The work force engaged in truly modern forms of industrial production was only 8 million. This means that 96 percent of the work force remained either in agriculture or, for the most part, in less mechanized sectors of the nonagricultural economy. (The source of the figures in this paragraph is the *Times of India Year-book*, 1969).

The primary sociological meaning of this is that the sectors of Indian society that have supported ascriptive occupational stratification, premodern technology, and traditional cultural values have survived and competed very actively with the modern economy and culture which the country's leaders have tried to promote. Villages are the bedrock of the caste system and of the type of Hinduism that validates it, and we have seen that 80 percent of the people continue to live in villages. The cities, too, are not centers of undiluted modernity. Vast reaches of most of them are really concentrations of people who have transplanted the essentials of peasant economic and social life to an urban setting. This concentration provides the votaries of traditional value systems with vast constituencies and cosmopolitan settings in which to develop opposition to rapid modernization.

The struggle between a new technology and associated way of life straining to be born and a very old and complex technology and associated way of life straining to survive provides a dramatic contemporary setting for better understanding the social structural transformations that industrialization caused in the West and is causing in most societies around the world today. We can observe in India the slow and uneven process by which old occupations have actually disappeared or become bureaucratized while new occupations were simultaneously coming into being by the widening bureaucratization of work. We can observe the changing functions of caste institutions under the impact of the growing bureaucratization of work even in those sectors of society where their survival has continued. We can gauge the relative importance of the forces of continuity and change directly and ascertain more accurately how much change in specific features of social structure is really demanded by the compulsions of the new technology. Singer concludes, for example, "that structural changes and structural persistence are not mutually exclusive phenomena, that both are occurring simultaneously" (Singer and Cohn, 1968, p. 438). This seems particularly true in transitional situations such as are found in developing nations today and were found in the West only yesterday.

As Kahl has said, "The occupational division of labor is the economically-determined skeleton on which the flesh of modern social organization develops; it is somewhat analogous in function to the kinship system that is the base of much of primitive society." We can, therefore, "use the division of labor as a convenient index of the degree of industrialization-urbanization reached by any given community" (Kahl, 1959, p. 18). Perhaps we can put this statement a little more precisely by saying that the measure of the progress of industrialization is the extent to which the occupational division of labor reveals occupations that emphasize performance qualities over ascriptive qualities and are integrated into bureaucratic structures.

In India today productive functions are rapidly losing their caste specificity, and castes are surviving insofar as their organizational principles find other applications. This process is most evident in the cities, of course, but it has penetrated the rural sector of society as well. Its presence in rural areas is due to the self-conscious efforts of the Indian government to change economic and social conditions in the countryside through community development programs, political reforms, and production incentives. It is also due to political forces for change that these policies have helped to unleash. Overall, the results seem to confirm further the generalizations of Marx and his successors about the inexorability of the social transformations wrought by industrialization.

We can see this more concretely by looking briefly at a few occupational categories in India. Because the caste system was primarily concerned with economic functions to which ritual implications were attributed, it can be said that all individual castes represented circumscribed bundles of productive skills. But because the functions and status of the different castes were considered hereditary, it also followed that each caste was, by and large, a closed corporate social segment, or for all practical purposes a type of ethnic group. Both these functional and ethnic attributes of Indian castes have proved transferable to the modernizing economy and social order in differing though not unrelated ways.

As for occupations, data from samples gathered in northern India during the 1960s clearly show a general relationship between traditional caste occupations and types of modern occupations reported.[5] Table 1 analyzes the contemporary occupations of 389 individuals from Lucknow, the capital of Uttar Pradesh, India's largest province. This sample consisted of 189 persons from economically successful families and 200 from families near or at the poverty level.[6] When the data are examined according to caste composition, it is at once clear that some mixture of caste and class traits determines occupational role and status in India today. Brahmans were always more than simply a guild of priests throughout Indian history; they were a literate class, advisors to kings and princes, teachers and philosophers, and recipients of innumerable economic favors from all walks of society.[7] Kayasthas and Vaidhs were traditional scribes and physicians respectively and also, therefore, suppliers of specialized functions to political and social elites. It seems less than accidental, therefore, that 63 percent of the Brahmans and 73 percent of the Kayasthas and Vaidhs in the sample pursued occupations in government and administration, science and technology, and academia. Kshatriyas, on the other hand, were supposed to be the traditional rulers. Their military might and proprietorship of the productive lands enabled them to govern the affairs of society. In historic times, tribes of Scythians who had invaded India during the centuries just preceding and following the beginning of the Christian era assimilated themselves to the Kshatriya status and came to be called Rajputs. Rajput *jatis* abound in northern India and continue to show powerful affinities to agricultural proprietorship, as Table 1 shows. Forty-nine percent of those in our sample retained this occupation. Vaisyas continued to show an equally strong

TABLE 1

Comparison of caste (or religion) with occupation of an economically differentiated sample of individuals in Lucknow, India

Type of occupation	Brahman (priest) N	%	Kshatriya (warrior) N	%	Kayastha/Vaidh (scribe, medic) N	%	Vaisya (merchant) N	%	Kisan (farmer) N	%	Artisan castes N	%	Impure castes N	%	Muslim religion N	%
1. Government and administration	8	24	3	8	12	26	18	21	—	—	—	—	—	—	1	1
2. Technical and scientific	9	27	3	8	15	32	14	16	—	—	—	—	—	—	—	—
3. Academic	4	12	2	5	7	15	4	5	—	—	—	—	—	—	1	1
4. Professional politics	—	—	3	8	—	—	—	—	—	—	—	—	—	—	—	—
5. Business enterprise	4	12	3	8	7	15	41	47	—	—	—	—	—	—	1	1
6. Petty service (government and private)	—	—	—	—	2	4	2	2	—	—	—	—	2	2	3	3
7. Petty shopkeeping	2	6	1	3	1	2	3	3	—	—	—	—	11	13	8	8
8. Agricultural proprietorship	4	12	18	49	2	4	3	3	—	—	—	—	—	—	—	—
9. Agricultural labor	—	—	—	—	—	—	—	—	8	100	—	—	8	10	—	—
10. Nonagricultural labor	—	—	3	8	—	—	1	1	—	—	7	78	44	54	63	66
11. Artisan work	—	—	—	—	1	2	—	—	—	—	2	22	17	21	18	19
12. Traditional occupations*	2	6	1	3	—	—	2	2	—	—	—	—	—	—	—	—
Total	33		37		47		88		8		9		82		95	

*Such as priest, curer, raja.

affinity to business enterprises, their traditional occupation. Artisans, kisans (or peasant farmers), and the defiled *jatis* were uniformly mired in rural or urban meniality. This was true of Muslim respondents as well, because they have been a severely depressed community since Islamic political power waned in the subcontinent.

But the table makes it clear that the transferability of occupations is not one-to-one. All of the modern occupations listed are controlled by the market and bureaucratized social structures, not by kinship structures legitimized by caste rules. Access to them has been conditioned by the residual attributes of the old castes. In the rush for modern occupations that accompanied the birth of an industrial age in India, those castes whose ritual status and traditional functions enabled their members to have a measure of economic power, literacy, and transferable economic skills enjoyed advantages over those that did not. British colonialism helped the old elite castes too, because as the colonial administration developed, it recruited Indians with exploitable abilities to help implement its policies (both Misra, 1961, and Seal, 1968, cast much empirical light on this aspect of Indian development under imperialism). Occupational histories of the well-to-do section of our sample reveal a consistent relationship between earlier recruitment into the colonial administration as a minor clerk or official and subsequent ability of a family to enter the modern social and economic order. Among the Vaisya or mercantile castes, however, the tendency was understandably less often to commence modern careers with government service and more often to transform a traditional enterprise into a modern one. Table 2 summarizes the time-dimensional aspects of movements into the modern economy.

Castes are not merely evaporating, however. Instead they are restructuring and consolidating themselves in order to perform important adaptive functions for their members in the context of the more open forms of social stratification now prevailing. As I put this some years ago, ". . . caste can be said to be in the process of becoming more and more explicitly an adaptive structure whose functions include the provision of security, solidarity and preferential treatment to groupings of people who seek to avoid the 'logical implications' of detailed

CASTE AND CLASS

universalistic discriminations, with respect to the competition for jobs and ...other scarce resources ..." (Gould' 1963, p. 431). Castes, in other words, are acting as co-optive instruments in the domain of access to jobs and social mobility. We see them acting in this way in both the productive and political sectors of Indian society. To the extent that given castes succeed in these efforts, their internal milieu takes on more and more of the attributes of a class system. That is, members acquire modern occupations in offices commanding differential wealth and prestige that radically affect life styles, educational standards and mobility patterns in the whole caste. Although this process has not as yet led to any serious abandonment of caste endogamy, it has resulted in more and more interaction between Indians along class lines. This is visible at both the top and the bottom of the status hierarchy.

TABLE 2

Occupational history of business and professional elite: generation in which first ancestor adopted modern occupation

Caste/community*	Ego's* generation	Ascending generations						Total
		1	2	3	4	5	Earlier	
Brahman	—	—	1	2	—	3	—	6
Rajput	1	2	1	—	—	—	—	4
Kayastha	—	—	1	2	—	—	1	4
Khatri	—	1	1	1	—	—	—	3
Sindhi	—	—	2	—	—	—	—	2
Baniya	1	1	—	1	—	—	—	3
Vaidh	—	—	1	—	—	—	—	1
Muslim	—	—	1	1	1	—	—	2
Christian	—	—	2	—	—	—	—	2
Total	2	4	10	7	—	3	1	27

*Ego = person interviewed.

Vast gaps have opened up in educational levels between the economicaly successful and unsuccessful, a typical development in industrializing societies, gaps that cleave the older homogeneities of caste. In the various samples available on Lucknow and its rural hinterland, the educational attainments of village Brahmans were found to be more similar to those of the general run of peasant farmers and menials and their urban counterparts than to those of wealthier urban Brahmans. In general, Table 3 clearly suggests that the educational profile of the members of elite castes (Brahman, Rajput, Kayastha, Vaidh, and Vaisya) whose families are in the upper echelons of the modern economic order markedly contrasts with that of their caste cohorts from villages. Conversely, the educational profile of the latter more nearly resembles that of rural farmers and menial castes.

A study of bicycle rickshaw drivers in Lucknow indicated that in ordinary urban menial occupations, common economic and functional lot produces considerable cross-caste social interaction without, however, leading to any breakdown of endogamy. A sample of 50 yielded an amazing variety of caste backgrounds: Brahmans (4), Rajputs (8), Jaiswaras (5), Kahars (4), Kurmis (1), Koris (2), Gujars (11), Muraos (2), Kumhars (1), Luniyas (1), Ahirs (1), and Valmiki Chamars (1)[8]. There were also 19 Muslims subdivided by "castes" and sects.

TABLE 3

Comparison of education attainments alof elite and lower castes differentiated by rural and urban backgrounds

Years of education	Villagers		Elite castes Urban business and professional		Lower castes Villagers	
	N	%	N	%	N	%
1-4	23	56.1	14	10.8	296	92.2
5-8	14	34.2	15	11.5	21	6.5
9-12	3	7.3	17	13.1	3	0.9
Interarts*	1	2.4	19	14.6	—	—
Bachelors	—	—	32	24.6	1	0.3
Masters	—	—	22	16.9	—	—
Doctorate	—	—	11	8.5	—	—
Total	41		130		321	

*Roughly equivalent to junior college in the United States.

On the job, these drivers mingled in every imaginable combination. They obviously saw their occupational functions and status as completely overriding the interactional strictures that caste placed on behavior in the traditional social order. Occupation had become completely "bureaucratized" in the sense of having become divorced from the control of heredity and the kin group.

Processes such as these undoubtedly characterized the transition from the medieval and ancient economies of Europe to the industrial economy of the nineteenth and early twentieth centuries. Guilds, regional communities, ethnic aggregates, sections of cities, feudal estates, etc., emphasized ascriptive characteristics in recruitment to and perpetuation of occupational functions. The difference between Europe and India was not in the technological base. It was, in part, one of degree and in part, of course, one of culture. Early Christianity did not emphasize the coterminousness of the division of labor and the division or ritual functions to the extent that Hinduism did. The ecclesiastical hierarchy of the Christian Church was itself somewhat "open" in that it separated role occupant from occupational role within the organization itself. Commoners could in principle rise to as high church offices as their moral and intellectual capacities allowed. The teachings of the church always had a strong measure of egalitarianism in them, a quality that increased over time, and this unquestionably helped promote a social climate where mobility could often be morally legitimated. The powerful commercial influences that the city states along the shores of the Mediterranean littoral, and later those of northern Europe, exerted on occupational proliferation and recruitment cannot be discounted as sources of contrast with India. But all-in-all, the types of social units in which the overwhelming mass of Europeans lived were broadly structurally analogous to the ascriptive social units in which Indians lived, and represented the same order of problem with respect to the changes that emerging industrialization would impose on them.

VII

In retrospect, we can say that the social foundations of both Eastern and Western civilization were laid when men in the Fertile Crescent invented the occupationalization of work and the stratification of occupations. They did so as a means of maximally exploiting the new relationships between technology and natural resources which they were gradually discovering. The consequences of their discoveries and inventions were vastly complex state systems in which not only unprecedented quantities of economic goods could be effectively produced, but immensly varied life styles, art and architectural forms, religions, philosophies, and political system could be created as well.

Among the network of civilizations that ramified outward from the Middle East and populated the Eurasiatic river valleys after 5000 B.C., India evolved a cultural system that carried the ascriptive principle for differentiating occupational roles to its ultimate expression. By modeling ritual behavior on the division of labor and ranking all occupational behavior on a pollution scale, Hinduism provided the basis for the virtually unlimited permutation of Indian society into hereditary compartments ordained to perform their separate but interdependent religious and economic functions. The caste system was the result.

The industrial revolution in the West, commencing in the eighteenth century A.D., enabled England, and subsequently other Western countries, to evolve a cultural system that applied the achievement principle to economic roles on a massive scale for the first time in human history. Occupational role and role-occupant were separated in principle by removing work from the control of kinship structures and placing that control in bureaucratic structures (factories) whose performance was controlled by the market. So-called developing societies like India are arenas where the two principles of social stratification (caste and class) compete and thereby dramatically reveal what are the essential properties of both.

NOTES AND REFERENCES

[1]Rawlinson (1937), Basham (1954), and Majumdar (1953) have written good basic histories of India.

CASTE AND CLASS

[2] Seleucus Nicator was one of Alexander's commanders who became ruler of the eastern remnants of the Persian Empire following the conqueror's death.

[3] The Vaisya *varna* includes all Twice-Born *jatis* that are not subsumed by the Brahman and Kshatriya *varnas*. See Gould, Chapter IV.

[4] The partial economic modernization of India is dealt with by a number of scholars. An early and still valuable study is one by Romesh Dutt (1956a, 1956b). Braibanti and Spengler (1953) have edited a volume of essays on the role of administration in econonmic development. Articles by Cohn (1960, 1970a, 1970b) and Morris (1960) on the modernization of the elite and the labor force respectively should be consulted.

[5] The field trips that yielded these data were those sponsored by the National Science Foundation and the National Institute of Mental Health.

[6] "Economically successful" families were defined as those possessing businesses or lands worth thousands of rupees, and/or whose head held a professional or administrative position affording major power over wealth or resources.

[7] Section I of *Traditional India: Structure and Change*, edited by Milton Singer (1959), contains articles which discuss the traditional conceptualizations of the major caste divisions in Hindu society. See especially Ingalls (1959).

[8] Jaiswaras are a subcaste of Chamars (leatherworkers); Kahars are water carriers; Kurmis are a cultivator caste of north India; Koris are cottonweavers; Gujars are an agricultural caste; Muraos are a caste of vegetable growers; Kumhars are potters; Luniyas are cultivators and growers; Ahirs are cowherders; and Valmikis are another subcaste of Chamars who have adopted the name of a medieval saint as their official appellation. Obviously, the disparity between traditional and present occupations bespeaks the kind of change that the introduction of a modern economy involves.

BIBLIOGRAPHY

Basham, A. L. (1954). *The Wonder that was India.* New York: Grove Press.

Berreman, Gerald D. (1960). "Caste in India and the United States." *American Journal of Sociology*, 66: 120-127.

Berreman, Gerald D. (1966). "Caste in Cross-Cultural Perspective: Organizational Components." In George DeVos and H. Wagatsuma eds., *Japan's Invisible Race: Caste in Culture and Personali.y*. Berkeley University of California Press.

Braibanti, Ralph, and Joseph J. Spengler, eds. (1963). *Administration and Economic Development in India.* Durham, N. C.: Duke University Press.

Chang, Chung-li (1955). *The Chinese Gentry*, Seattle: University of

Washington Press.
Childe, V. Gordon (1942). *What Happened in History*: Harmondsworth: Penguin Books
Childe, V. Gordon (1951). *Man Makes Himself*. New York: New American Library (Mentor Books).
Cohn, Bernard S. (1960). The Initial British Impact on India." *The Journal of Asian Studies*, 19: 418-431,
Cohn, Bernard S. (1970b). "Society and Social Change under the Raj." *South Asian Review*, 4: 27-49.
Cohn, Bernard S. (1970a). "Recruitment of Elites in India Under British Rule." In Leonard Plotnicov and Arthur Tuden, eds., *Essays in Comparative Social Stratification*. Pittsburgh: University of Pittsburgh Press.
Davis, Kingsley (1951). *The Population of India and Pakistan*. Princeton N.J.: Princeton University Press.
Dumont, Louis (1961). "Caste, Racism and 'Stratification'." In Louis Dumont and David Pocock, eds., *Contributions to Indian Sociology*, No. V, pp. 20-43. The Hague- Mouton.
Dumont, Louis (1965). "The Modern Conception of the Individual." In Louis Dumont and David Pocock, eds., *Contributions to Indian Sociology*, No, VIII, pp. 13-61. The Hague. Mouton.
Dumont, Louis, and David Pocock (1957). "For a Sociology of India." In Louis Dumont and David Pocock, eds., *Contributions to Indian Sociology*, No. I, pp. 7-22. The Hague: Mouton.
Dumont, Louis, and David Pocock (1959). "Pure and Impure." In Louis Dumont and David Pocock, eds., *Contributions to Indian Sociology*, No. III, pp. 9-39. The Hague: Mouton.
Dutt, Romesh (1956a). *The Economic History of India Under Early British Rule*. London: Routledge and Kegan Paul.
Dutt, Romesh (1956b). *The Economic History of India in the Victorian Age*. London: Routledge and Kegan Paul.
Eliade, Mircea (1964). *Shamanism: Archaic Techniques of Ecstasy*. New York: Pantheon Books.
Gould, Harold A. (1963). "The Adaptive Functions of Caste in Contemporary Indian Society." *Asian Survey*, 3: 427-438.
Gould, Harold A. (1964), "A Jajmani System of North India: its Structure, Magnitude and Meaning." *Ethnology*, 3: 12-41.
Gould, Harold A. (1965). "Lucknow Rickshawallas: the Social Organization of an Occupational Category." In K. Ishwaran and Ralph Piddington, eds, *Kinship and Geographical Mobility* Leiden: E J. Brill.
Gould, Harold A. (1967). "Priest and Contrapriest: a Structural Analysis of Jajmani Relationships in the Hindu Plains and Nilgiri Hills." In Contributions to Indian Sociology, New Series, No. 1, pp. 26-55, New York: Asian Publishing House (Also, Chapter IV of this volume).
Hardgrave, Robert L., Jr. (1969). "The New Mythology of a Caste in Change " *Journal of Jamil Studies*, 1: 1-25.
Harpar, Edward B. (1968). "A Comparative Analysis of Caste: the

United States and India." In Milton Singer and Bernard S. Cohn, eds., *Structure and Change in Indian Society*. Chicago: Aldine.
Hocart, A. M. (1950). *Caste, a Comparative Study*. London: Methuen
Hutton, J. H. (1963). *Caste in India: its Nature, Function, and Origins*. New York: Oxford University Press.
Ingalls, Daniel (1959). "The Brahman Tradition." In Milton Singer, ed., *Traditional India: Structure and Change*. Philadelphia: American Folklore Society.
Jackson, A. V. Williams (1907). *History of India*, 9 vols. New York: Grolier Society.
Kahl, Joseph A. (1959). "Some Social Concomitants of Industrialization: a Research Review." *Human Organization*, 18: 53-74.
Kolenda, Pauline M. (1963). "Toward a Model of the Jajmani System." *Human Organization*, 22: 11-31.
Leach, E. R. (1960). "Introduction: What Should We Mean by Caste" In E. R. Leach, ed., *Aspects of Caste in South India, Ceylon and Northwest Pakistan*. Cambridge: Cambridge University Press.
Lévi-Strauss, Claude (1963), "The Bear and the Barber." *Journal of the Royal Anthropological Society*, 93: 1-11.
Linton, Ralph (1964). *The Study of Man*. New York, Appleton-Century Crofts.
Lipset, Seymour Martin, and Reinhard Bendix (1959). *Social Mobility in Industrial Society*. London: Heinemann.
Majumdar, R. D., et al. (1953). *An Advanced History of India*. New York: Macmillan.
Marx, Karl (1951). *Articles on India*. Peoples Publishing House.
Merton, Robert F. (1958). *Social Theory and Social Structure*. New York Free Press.
Misra, B. B. (1961). *The Indian Middle Classes: their Growth in Modern Times*. New York: Oxford University Press.
Morris, Morris David (1960). "Caste and the Evolution of the Industrial Workforce in India." *Proceedings of the American Philosophical Society*. 104: 124-133.
Myrdal, Gunnar (1942). *An American Dilemma*. New York: Harper.
Nadel, S. F. (1954). "Caste and Government in Primitive Society." *Journal of the Anthropological Society of Bombay*, 8: 9-22.
Nehru, Jawaharlal (1954). *Speeches*. New Delhi: Publications Division, Government of India.
Orenstein, Henry (1968). "Toward a Grammar of Defilement in Hindu Sacred Law." In Milton Singer and Bernard S. Cohn, eds., *Structure and Change in Indian Society* Chicago: Aldine.
Parsons, Talcott (1952). *The Social System*. New York: Free Press.
Piggott, Stuart (1950). *Prehistoric India*. Harmondsworth: Penguin Books
Pusalker, A. D (1957). "The Indus Valley Civilization." In R. C. Majumdar, *The Vedic Age*. London: George Allen and Unwin.
Rawlinson, H. G. (1937). *India, a Short Cultural History*. New York: Praeger.

Renou, Louis, ed. (1963). *Hinduism.* New York: Washington Square Press.
Rowe, John Howland (1965). "The Renaissance Foundations of Anthropology." *American Anthropologist,* 67: 1-20.
Rudolph, Lloyd, and Susanne Rudolph (1967). *The Modernity of Tradition: Political Development in India.* Chicago: University of Chicago Press.
Sahlins, Marshall D. (1958). *Social Stratification in Polynesia.* Seattle University of Washington Press.
Seal, Anil (1968). *The Emergence of Indian Nationalism.* Cambridge: Cambridge University Press.
Singer, Milton. ed. (1959). *Traditional India: Structure and Change.* Philadelphia: American Folklore Society.
Singer, Milton, and Bernard S. Cohn, eds. (1968). *Structure and Change in Indian Society* Chicago: Aldine.
Sjoberg, Gideon S. (1960). *The Preindustrial City.* New York: Free Press.
Srinivas, M. N. (1962). *Caste in Modern India and Other Essays.* New York: Asia Publishing House.
Srinivas, M. N. (1966). *Social Change in Modern India.* Berkeley: University of California Press.
Warner, W. Lloyd, et al. (1949). *Social Class in America.* Social Science Associates.
Wheeler. Sir Mortimer (1966). *Civilizations of the Indus Valley and Beyond* London: Thames and Hudson.
Wiser, William (1936). *The Hindu Jajmani System.* Lucknow: Lucknow Publishing House.
Wolf, Eric R. (1966). *Peasants.* Englewood Cliffs, N.J.: Prentice-Hall.

3

Castes, Outcastes and the Sociology of Stratification

I

India is well-recognized as a society where are to be found those most striking of all social categories, the pariah castes, the Untouchables, whose occupations are regarded as so polluting, so morally defiling that their practitioners must be kept segregated as much as possible from other members of society.[1] What is not so well-recognized, however, is that certain other Asian countries have possessed social groups which bear a close resemblance to India's Untouchables. Furthermore, in many parts of the world, both in the past and in the present one finds numerous cases where systems of social stratification are sufficiently rigid to involve some suggestion of untouchability where not the institution in its full state of development. Instances of what may be called genuine untouchability on the Indian model include the Eta or Buraku of Japan, the Paekchong of Korea and the Ragyappa of Tibet.[2] Ceylon has always known untouchability in fact if not in principle,[3] and historically speaking, untouchable-like groups have been recorded in China and Burma.[4] Instances outside Asia where stratification systems have generated groups possessing some of the attributes of untouchability are widely dispersed around the world; they include such divergent cultural environments as the American South, Polynesia, sub Saharan Africa, ancient and Medieval Europe, and Latin America.[5] In a very real sense, 19th Century colonialism often created caste-like divisions between the European administrators and settlers, on the one hand, who managed and economically profited from it, and the indigenous populations who were its victims, on the other. South Africa's racial caste system, in which the Black has been compelled to assume many of the social characteristics of pariah status, is a direct cultural outgrowth of colonialism.

In this paper[6] an attempt will be made to explore, in necessarily preliminary terms, the reasons for the occurrence of caste structures, and their most extreme manifestations, untouchable groups, in so many different places and in so many different sociocultural contexts. Obviously, unless one is prepared to believe in multiple cases of unique social causation, societies displaying caste characteristics may be suspected of having some structural properties in common which predispose them to develop along such lines once the right combination of historical events occurs.

II

Viewed from the standpoint of the obviously very wide prevalence of socially excluded communities, it is clear that in the study of caste groups we are concerned simply with a particular aspect of the study of social stratification. And since social stratification is to be found in all human communities above a certain level of technological scale,[7] our task is to distinguish the forms of social stratification which contain the phenomena in which we are interested from those which do not. At the outset, it must be realized that the term 'outcaste' is actually misleading in its implications. Outcastes are, of course, actually a variety of *caste group*. Their presence in a society announces that caste in one of its more extreme manifestations is to be found there. In the case of Asia, I would contend, their presence further announces that a particular mingling has occurred between a certain general type of social stratification and certain notions concerning purity and pollution which emanate from India and which have penetrated the institutions of other Asian societies by the process of cultural diffusion.

To commence with some necessary definitions, social stratification is the formation of clusters of individual work or other functional roles into a ranked system of work (or other functional) categories. Stratification takes place whenever a society grows so complex that work[8] becomes *occupational* (i.e., specialized) in character and the number of occupational roles becomes so great that discreet discriminations cannot be made any longer between each for purposes of assigning rewards and prestige.[9] Roles become part of a category of roles whose reward and prestige value in the society are approximately the same; in other words, they form a social stratum whose position is to be understood in relation to other strata[10] consisting of other similarly clustered social roles of different rank. People occupying these social roles, and their kin, experience one another in their social interaction with greater frequency than they do the occupants of social roles lodged in other strata and, as well, come to have certain common perceptions of the overall social order due to their similar general position and reward-level in it. In other words, the occupants of occupational roles in a given stratum of society come to form a *subcultural system* with an empirically differentiable standard of living, moral outlook, level and type of education, socialization pattern, etc. The uniformity and rigidity of such subcultural variation in turn depends heavily upon whether a society's stratification system allocates occupational roles on the basis of ascriptive or achievement criteria. In the former case, role and role-occupant tend to be merged into a single qualitative entity whereas in the latter a distinction is made between the occupant of a role and the role itself. The type of stratification system in which a person and occupational role are a single qualitative entity we may call *ascription-oriented*; the type of social stratification system in which a distinction is made between person and occupational role we may call *achievement-oriented*.

Obviously, the main reason for this difference is the inclination to inhibit social mobility in the ascription-oriented stratification system and to encourage it (within limits at least) in the achievement-oriented system. This makes a considerable difference in the nature and degree of subcultural development one finds in relation to the occupational strata which each system generates. Broadly speaking, the former is inclined to be more accommodative in character while the latter is inclined to be more assimilative. That is, ascription-oriented stratification systems basically leave intact the general social organization of the constituent groups making up the society. Occupational specialization and differentation are merely made coterminous with these constituent groups. The groups may be, and in traditional societies usually are, highly varied in their ethnic characteristics, culture and social organization. The members of these groups tend to inherit the occupational contribution (or complex of contributions) they make to the division of labor in society through the descent system which is characteristic of their respective groups.[11] Achievement-oriented stratification systems are more disruptive of the general social organization of constituent groups in the society because here occupations are removed from the control of descent systems and placed under the control of bureaucratic social structures where a more or less standardized set of criteria (merit, educalion, ability) determine functions in the productive system and duration of stay at any given level of it.

Each of the two forms of social stratification has tended to be associated with a particular kind of society—the ascriptive type with non-industrial state systems and the achievement type with industrialized states. This is also crucial for understanding the formation of caste groups because caste, being simply an extreme manifestation of ascription-oriented stratification can, in my opinion, originate only in non-industrial societies (although once in existence they may 'carry over' into an industrial society, especially during the nascent stages of the latter's emergence). In their pure forms, however, each type would be mutually exclusive of the other and, although the pure expression of either would be impossible in social reality wherever industrialization has reached highly advanced stages of development, occupational groups with ascribed status have tended to be sharply reduced in their number and importance. On the other hand, the large-scale 'traditional' societies (i.e., nonindustrial complex societies) have revealed only the most limited tendencies to dissociate the status of persons from the status of the work which they do.[12]

With these observations in mind concerning the characteristics of social stratification as I view them, let us now examine some of the features of nonindustrial societies which predispose them toward the development of ascription-oriented stratification systems in general and caste groups in particular.

(1) In non-industrial societies, technology is based upon manual and animal energy and productive activities are performed in kinship groups.[13] This means that occupations are part of the intrafamilial socialization process and are thus internalized as an intrinsic part of the parent-child relationship. Occupations are 'inherited' at birth, are believed to be transmitted in the 'blood'line,' and are therefore seen as part of the person.

(2) The ruling group is usually an elite who believe and teach that their status is divinely ordained and mystically preserved. Much of their official duties consist of performing or overseeing rituals which stress the sacrosanctness of their position in contrast to the morally inferior position of their subjects. Sometimes the traditional elite are bifurcated to form two strata, each of which specializes in different dimensions of the elitist role. That is, the priestly and ritual functions of traditional elite status get vested in a stratum of religious specialists while the political and military functions of the status become identified with a stratum of dynasts. This, of course, is the structural foundation of the Brahman Kshatriya symbiosis found in Indian civilization. In any case, political power in ascription-oriented societies, whatever may be their specific mode of institutional integration, tends to be autocratic in form and hereditary in transmission.

(3) Whether coterminous with royal power or not, specialists in religious and ritual practices are key agents in formulating the values and setting the moral tone which dominate the traditional, ascription-oriented society. Their chief function is to harmonize man and society with the cosmic order, to sacramentalize the *status quo* which is regarded as timeless and fundamentally unalterable. A conception of the division of labor as determined by heredity accords well with such a conservative viewpoint.

(4) The urban centers of these societies house the sacred elite, religious and administrative groups, the numerous other specialists who cater to the needs of civilized consumers, and the various menial groups who perform necessary unskilled tasks. These cities embrace a comparatively small proportion of the nonindustrial society's total population (less than 20%) and

they survive by their ability to expropriate the surpluses created under administrative compulsion by the majority living in small agricultural communities.

(5) Peasant village communities contain the bulk of the nonindustrial society's population. They consist of small clusters of kinship groups (usually but not always corporate in nature)[11] which produce food by manual labor, animal power and a generally crude technology for their own consumption and for the market. Consisting of limited numbers of kin groups, peasant villages are marked by personal, face-to-face relationships which facilitate easy determination of identity and thus of status.[15] This is one of the most crucial factors in the causation and perpetuation of ascriptive-oriented stratification systems.

III

Thus, ascription-oriented stratification systems are found in societies where occupations are rooted in kinship structures, where urban development is limited in quality and quantity by this fact (because most productive activities are dispersed in countless rural communities whose primary concern is local subsistence) and where sacramentalism and political absolutism are the primary means employed by ruling elites to legitimize and perpetuate their preeminent position in the social order. Together, these conditions mean the virtual nonexistence of occupational mobility in the modern sense and the forcing of occupations into heredity molds. Occupational strata resultantly tend to be associated with groups of people who are perennially identified with and evaluated by the work they do. Should events occur in such societies which involve a sharp intensification of the moral significance assigned to hereditary occupational distinctions, the result is the emergence of true, ritualized caste structures. Primarily, such an occurrence requires the development of a *religion*, or so I would assert, which lays emphasis upon the idea that the division of labor is not only determined by hereditary criteria of recruitment, but that its hierarchical arrangement is *prima facie* a statement of the different amounts of moral worth possessed by the different members of society. Linked to this moral judgement concerning the occupational order there arises an ethical dictum that the spiritual well-being of the various social groups thereby delimited requires that they practice elaborate patterns of marital endogamy and social exclusivism. We may call this the occurrence of a *caste ethic*.

The operation of a caste ethic makes entirely understandable the existence of so-called outcaste groups.[16] When the occupational order is made the basis for the moral hierarchization of society, purity for the superordinate strata can be had only at the expense of impurity for the subordinate strata. This is the case because occupations adjudged morally inferior are just as essential to the successful operation of the society as are those adjudged morally superior.[17] When seen in the context of the nonindustrial society, this is especially important because most of the population lives in peasant communities where the quest for maximal self-sufficiency is a paramount consideration. When the caste ethic of a society prescribes for some of its members occupational functions essential to the performance of agriculture, say, or to community sanitation, then in each such community the persons who perform these occupations must absorb the onus of moral reprehensibility connected with them; but they must perform them nevertheless because someone must do so if the community is to function at all. In my opinion, this is the fundamental social 'dilemma', so to speak, of the caste society; it is of necessity resolved by putting certain groups identified with impure occupations in the position of being simultaneously outside the pale ritually yet inside the pale functionally. This is achieved not by *ostracising* the practitioners of such occupations from the community but *circumscribing their range and type of social interaction* in whatever way and to whatever degree the dominant and 'pure' groups in the society believe is necessary to 'protect' themselves from 'contamination'. We are speaking here of course, of the extreme manifestations of the dilemma in which pariah castes occur which are subjected to maximum amounts of social avoidance and circumscription. But the general principle holds in any society where the caste ethnic is to be found in any significant measure.

Non-industrial societies confronted with problems of multi-ethnic integration seem to be particularly prone to the evolution of a caste ethic.[28] India, the caste society *par excellence*, is also a classic case of ethnic variety. Since the dawning of Bronze

Age a two-fold process of accommodation has taken place there. On the one hand, there has been a constant flow of peoples through the northwest passes out onto the Hindustan Plain and thence into all reaches of the country. On the other hand, there has been a continuous percolation of indiginous tribal peoples into the ambit of Indian Civilization. Groups in the former category have tended to stabilize into strata controlling privileged occupations because they have normally come into India as conquerors able to enforce their status pretentions. Aboriginals have tended to stabilize into strata embracing the defiled and degraded occupations because they have lacked the political power to facilitate claims to higher status. The aboriginals are mainly variants of the Austroasiatic racial stock whereas the Steppe peoples who have entered India have been primarily Caucasoids and secondarily Mongoloids.

Thus, there are to be found in the various regions of India continua of racial and cultural characteristics which roughly correspond to the specific complex of accommodation that has historically occurred there. To a degree, Hinduism seems to represent the evolution of a moral-ethical system which has elaborately reconciled on an accommodative basis the great variety of peoples who have come to make up the society sufficiently to permit their integration into the pattern of nonindustrial civilization. This has been achieved, in general, by ratifying in ritual or *morally intrinsic* terms the position in the division of labor which the political and technological characteristics of given groups enabled them to assume relative to others.

In many other caste situations, similar problems of accomodation have arisen and seem to have been resolved along similar lines. The fact that such contact situations occur in the context of nonindustrial societies where ascription-oriented stratification systems are the social structural mode is in my view a most important variable in this. Another important variable is the fact that conquerors are normally a numerically inferior group with superior military and political power. Lacking the capacity to absorb the conquered into their own cultural mold, they must on the contrary devise ways of avoiding being themselves absorbed by the majority whom they rule. By adopting and enforcing a conception of society which sees every perceived stratum as fixed in status and as a reflection of the differential moral worth of people, i.e., by formulating a caste ethnic, this end can be accomplished.

But an ethnic interpretation will not by itself account for all the instances of observable caste structures, even in societies where it can be shown that such factors have indeed played a major part in their development. It certainly will not account for all the caste variety found in India. Although some high caste north Indian groups show distinctly Caucasian physical traits and many low caste north Indian groups are unmistakably Austroasiatic in racial origins, Ghurye observes that in general, "Brahmans of each of the linguistic areas show greater physical affinity with other castes of their region than with the Brahmans of other areas and of Hindustan."[19] The rigidities inherent in the occupational stratification system of the nonindustrial form of society are really quite sufficient in themselves to engender attitudes of difference between the various occupationalized strata that are comparable in their intensity to those which often occur as a result of multi-ethnic contact. Where the two operate in concert, the foundation is laid for the most elaborate expressions of the caste ethic.[20] This would seem to be one of the most important bases for India's classic position among the caste societies of the world. But the ethnic factor is not essential to such developments, I feel. Empirically it is a matter of determining in each separate case what specifically led to the formation of a caste ethic out of the cultural and social structural material available. Quite likely it will be discovered that in some instances for example, groups with pariah status have had attributed to them an alien origin by folk mythology when in fact no such alien origin can actually be proved. A highly developed concept of 'difference'[21] can easily lead to ideas that those who do reprehensible and defiling work are so outside the pale that they must have different racial origins than the ordinary members of society. In this connection, Passin observes in the case of Korean, Tibetan and Japanese untouchables that:

> Whatever the actual historical facts may be, their separation from society is often attributed to their alleged alien origin. These popular attributions express the feeling that outcastes are so different from oneself that they must be of a different race.[22]

IV

Let us turn now to the phenomenon of outcaste groups in various parts of Asia, for here we find one of the most striking manifestations of the emergence of the caste ethic in lands outside India. It is desirable to consider these first because their nature makes it clear that Indian Civilization played an indirect role in their development. In learning the nature of this role it will be possible to observe how a set of indigenous developments in each society were catalyzed, as it were, by cultural diffusion until a caste ethic strong enough to generate a stratum of occupational roles possessing pariah status was the result.

The societies which besides India have in their history experienced the development of clearly untouchable groups are Korea, Japan and Tibet. In Korea this category was called the Paekchong, in Japan it was known as the Eta or Buraku, and in Tibet it was known as the Ragyappa. All had in common the fact that they consisted of people whose occupational roles involved them in activities which from the standpoint of their respective cultures made them morally impure and thus simultaneously outside the ritual pale of their society yet essential to its proper functioning, technologically speaking.

Both the Paekchong and the Eta were thought to be impure because their work dealt with the slaughtering of animals and the tanning of hides. The Eta were responsible for the removal of dead animals and human bodies and for the removal of dirt. On this account, these two groups had to live in separated sections of the community, removed as much as possible from the possibility of defiling contacts with the 'clean' members of society. They were compelled to practice endogamy and were in general not considered worthy of being accorded the usual civil guarantees. One could not eat with them, go to their homes or have any ordinary social intercourse with them. In all these respects the position of the Paekchong and the Eta was equivalent to the status of Untouchables in India. And what is most important, the categories of occupational roles for which outcaste status was assigned were fundamentally the same as in India. People who killed animals, removed their carcasses, made leather products, or removed dirt, or, as Passin puts it, were associated with "blood, death and dirt", were adjudged outside the moral pale in all three places.[23]

The Ragyappa of Tibet were scavengers and animal slaughterers and were responsible for clearing away carcasses. Some categories of Ragyappa were also responsible for breaking up the corpses of deceased monks for feeding to the vultures—a special trait of Tibetan Buddhism. This caste group was compelled to live on the outskirts of Lhasa, practice endogamy, and was held to be morally reprehensible and ritually dangerous. Yet, like the Eta and the Paekchong, as well as India's Untouchables, the work done by the Ragyappa was indispensable to Tibetan society, given its cultural premises; the caste was functionally wholly within the pale despite being ritually outside it. They spared the orthodox, high status Tibetans from moral contamination by themselves absorbing the onus of ritual impurity; in exchange they enjoyed whatever economic advantages accrued from having an assured monopoly over their occupations.

According to Hutton,[24] there was a time in Burmese history when pagoda slaves were regarded as pariahs but this was apparently not because they had anything to do with dead organisms or other 'dirty' occupations in the Indian sense. Perhaps the significant fact is that some kind of concept of untouchability existed in Burma even though somewhat different in its content. We will turn a little later to the question of how this phenomenon might have come about. Meanwhile, let us note that throughout Southeast Asia there is evidence of there having been a much more weakly developed caste ethic despite obvious and long-standing cultural contacts with nearby India. Bali is to some extent an exception to this in the sense that a form of avowed Hinduism exists there replete with caste structures. However these castes are not identical to those found in India.

Ceylon has caste and outcaste groups in fact but no formally proclaimed caste system. In general, it may be said that Ceylon clearly has a well-entrenched caste ethic but for a number of reasons, one being the dominance of Buddhism, far less manifest than in India. Thus, in the overall, it would seem that to the north and northeast of India there is evidence of the occurrence of untouchability in forms extremely analogous to that found in India, while to the south and southeast there is evidence of a much milder development of such caste structures on the Indian model.

Throughout the entire region we have been considering, nonindustrial urban society began penetrating by 3,000 B.C., and was universally well-established by 1,000 A.D. The first civilization in this area came to northwestern India; either it came by cultural diffusion of the basic technological patterns from Mesopotamia or else it developed partially independently and then got accelerated and elaborated by contact with the former. This is, of course, the famous Indus Valley Civilization whose great cities of Harappa and Mohenjo-daro indicate the existence of a highly differentiated population, extensive and powerful religious and political elites, and a vast hinterland of lesser cities, towns and agricultural villages. Undoubtedly this is the foundation upon which Indian Civilization arose. Among the excavated sites from which our knowledge of this Civilization comes have been discovered great bathing centers suggesting an early concern with ritual cleansing; also terracotta seals imprinted with typical symbols of later Hinduism like the cobra, the Brahma bull, and holy men sitting in the yoga posture.[25]

Excavations make it plain that a stratified system of occupations existed. Not only does the architecture and lay-out of the cities, and the fact that such elaborate material culture could not have been achieved in the absence of specialists, suggest this but also studies of the neolithic villages integrated into the economy of the Civilization suggest it; for some appear to have been specialized in supplying only one or two commodities to the urban centers.[26]

At this stage it is virtually certain that occupational roles and their practitioners were defined as a single qualitative entity and that stratification was resultantly ascription-oriented. Since no translatable writing has ever been discovered we cannot be sure whether a true caste ethic had made any of the occupational strata morally intrinsic. The existence of structures which must have been palaces, others which must have housed prosperous subordinates of high authority, others which must have domiciled some sort of priesthood or professional ritualists, and so on, down to structures which obviously betray menial status tell us that some kind of royal power was operative and that occupational hierarchy and the proto-Hindu symbolic materials lean towards the hypothesis that some idea of ritual purity was operative, and therefore that a caste ethic might have already arisen. But nothing can be said for certain about its nature and range of applicability.

At any rate, the coming of the so-called Aryans around 1,500 B.C. heralds the commencement of conditions in India which lead directly to the creation of a highly variegated system of castes. The chief impetus seems to have been supplied by the Aryans themselves who were either genuinely racially different from the indigenous population (an unlikely probability) or else regarded themselves as such and therefore created a set of cultural rationalizations which legitimized their self-perception. The Hindu religious classics reveal a gradual crystalization of a caste ethic which divides society into a hierarchy of four morally intrinsic, occupationally-specific strata: Priests (*Brahmans*), Warriors and Rulers (*Kshatriyas*), Traders, Artisans and Cultivators (*Vaishyas*), and Menials (*Sudras*). Untouchables, or *Tchandalas*, were basically a substratum of *Sudra* occupational groups (*jatis*) whose work entailed the most pervasive contact with 'blood, death and dirt'.[27] Ideally, then, the system which emerged consisted of a priestly caste whose primary functions were ritual and sacerdotal, whose moral sanctity could be preserved only by the avoidance of numerous varyingly impure tasks whose onus, therefore, had to be born by other social groups (the other *Varnas* and their *jatis*) whose moral status was evaluated accordingly. As noted earlier, as the caste ethic developed in India, and morally intrinsic occupational groups formed one after another, their hierarchical arrangement reflected their relative socioeconomic power. Aboriginals consistently remained in the lower categories of the caste order since their hunting and gathering economies yielded them neither the power, the numbers nor the skills necessary to challenge the technologically and culturally more advanced people who filtered through the Khyber Pass or who had already established themselves in the urban centers.

As already noted, religious and secular power early became

bifurcated in the Indian Civilization between Brahmans and Kshatriyas. Some feel that this bifurcation was an important manifestation of patterns of rivalry between dominant elites in India which eventually led to the emergence of Buddhism.[29] Whether or not this is actually so, it is nevertheless true that the historic Buddha was a Kshatriya who was reared in the foothills of the Himalayas along the northern periphery of Hindustan and who founded a religion which clearly challenged the supremacy of the Brahman schools of ritual mysticism which had enjoyed uncontested supremacy in the cultural centers of ancient Magadha and Kosala. The essence of early Buddhism seems to have been an attempt to modify the ritual and doctrinal rigors of Brahmanism and to thereby make a wider segment of mankind eligible to strive for and achieve spiritual enlightenment.

Caste distinctions were played down by early Theravada and related Buddhist doctrines, which came to be called the Hinayana. By the fourth century B.C. the new religion had grown sufficiently important to become the personal creed of the Mauryan Emperor Ashoka, and to form a major component of the religious synthesis, compounded of Brahmanism, Buddhism, and Jainism, which he attempted to make the moral-ethical basis of his vast empire. On his Rock Edicts, Ashoka published the fruits of this distillation, as illustrated by the following quotations from two of them:

Rock Edict No. 1:
1. *No animal may be slaughtered for sacrifice.*
2. Tribal feasts are not to be celebrated.
3. Docility to parents is good.
4. Liberality to friends, acquaintances and relatives and to Brahmans and recluses is good.

Rock Edict No. 2:
5. *Not to injure living things. This is good.*
6. Economy in expenditure, and avoiding disputes is good.[29]

By the beginning of the Christian era, Buddhism had come

full-cycle. Having had centuries to grow and develop and enjoy patronization by several Indian dynasties, it had acquired more and more elaborate rites, doctrines and physical wealth and had become far removed from the rather elemental ethical credo originally propounded by Buddha. And what is essential in this from the standpoint of our discussion is that the modifications undergone by Buddhism made it emerge doctrinally much closer to the original Hinduism from which it parturated. The Mahayanna, or 'Great Vehicle,' which officially came into being after the council of Kashmir, held during the reign of the Kushana King, Kanishka (120-142 A.D.), had taken over from Hinduism the doctrine of *avatara* (multiple incarnations of the Divine Being), the doctrine of the World Soul (*Atman*), and numerous other items which the historical Buddha had rejected or played down.[30] And perhaps what is most crucial of all from the standpoint of Buddhism's role in helping to generate caste ethics in other parts of Asia (for such is the assertion of this essay) is that both of its forms retained the Hindu abhorrence for doing violence to living things (*Ahimsa*). But before going farther, it is necessary to examine the pattern of development in nonindustrial society in the rest of the Far East.

The other great center of Farther Asian civilization was China. A neolithic phase was dawning along the Hwang Ho by at least 3,000 B.C. and the idea of urban life, along with the metalurgical and other specializations upon which it was based, had spread to the region by the middle of the second milennium B.C.[31] Out of these beginnings emerged the great sequence of Chinese dynasties which produced a civilization rooted, like all nonindustrial civilizations, in a peasant economy but crowned with one of the most remarkable administrative systems achieved in antiquity. The imperial political system in China was based on sacerdotal absolu ism which conceived of the emperor as a supreme and unquestioned ruler responsible for performing rituals assuring the health, tranquility and productivity of the realm. But the great bureaucratic system which supplied Chinese dynasties with the administrative structure and professional personnel capable of mobilizing and utilizing vast human and material resources in the service of the state was remarkably atypical of nonindustrial societies in general, in the degree to which it was achievement-oriented.[32]

Although there were well-developed tendencies toward fusing persons with their occupational roles in other domains of technology, the civil service separated person and work-role to the extent that individuals could advance to new positions if their performance on the Confucian examinations warranted it. In reality, however, even entry into the bureaucracy was confined almost exclusively to one stratum of society, the Gentry, because literacy was presupposed as a condition of candidacy—a condition which this group alone could consistently fulfill but which other groups, like the peasantry, rarely could.

In addition to supplying ethical canons for a 'merit system' of bureaucratic mobility, the Confucian ethic (formulated by Confucius about the same time that Buddha formulated his in India) supplied justification for deposing an emperor whenever natural calamities or national disasters reached a magnitude which suggested that he was lacking in virtue and thereby unable to fulfill his sacerdotal obligations. Thus, the core 'ethic' of Chinese Civilization contained features which could be said to be fundamentally opposed to a typical caste ethic such as the one Buddhism propagated. This is an important point to keep in mind when considering the question of Buddhism's impact on Chinese Civilization.

Both Korea and Japan got their basic social structure and technology from the Chinese mainland by cultural diffusion. Yet neither took the Confucian ethic in a form which led to achievement-oriented patterns of administrative recruitment nor to political skepticism. Their imperial systems were much more the usual types of sacerdotal absolutisms which have marked most nonindustrial societies. Occupational stratification was predominantly ascription-oriented.

Japan, in addition, had the doctrine of Shintoism which, as Sansom (1955) puts it, sees "the universe as composed of myriad sentient parts, a nature worship of which the mainspring was appreciation rather than fear and an ancestor worship that springs from...the sun goddess." He goes on to say:

As one might expect, in a cult so concerned with nature, most of its observances have to do with growth and decay. Growth is good and decay is evil, life is desirable, death is abominable. So we find on the one hand prayers and thanksgiving for the harvest or the birth of a child, and on the other hand a severe ritual to guard against or to wash away the pollution of sickness and mortality. It is in this that the Shinto cult develops rituals of purification, gratification and worship so similar to the rituals developed under the influence of the Hindu pantheon...[33]

In short, Shintoist Japan had the kernel of a caste ethic in the pre-Buddhist period of her history. It was upon this indigenous cult that incoming Buddhism impacted. Pre-Buddhist Korea also revealed tendencies to equate moral condition with occupational status, but the record is not as clear as for Japan. Observes Passin:

> There was...already inherent in the early Confucianism of Korea a predisposition to consider that the lower the occupation, the more immoral, the more lacking in virtue, it was.[34]

Civilization dawned considerably later in Southeast Asia than it did in India and China, and many aspects of its occurrence there are still imperfectly understood. A separate system of rice cultivation seems to have developed in Southeast Asia sometime before the Christian era and formed part of a distinctive neolithic complex in the region. When urban systems came into being they show evidence of considerable borrowing from the Indic world. Both Brahmanism and Buddhism impacted there, clearly in the context of extensive maritime interaction between the eastern coast of India and the lands of "Farther India." The technological base of these cultures was comparable in scale and complexity to what has been found to be typical of nonindustrial societies generally in Eurasia.

Tibet got patterns of civilization as a by-product of her position athwart the trade routes coursing between the Far East and the rimland regions of South and Southwest Asia. These patterns were meagre by comparison with other regions and sufficient to give rise to only a few genuinely civilized (i.e., urban) loci, such as Lhasa and Shigatse and one or two others.[36] The country is too poor in soil and too mountainous to have sustained a massive nonindustrial society. Thus, Tibetan society really comprised a few cities of limited complexity housing ascetic bodies professing a variety of Buddhism interlarded with substantial shamanic elements, and surrounded by a nomadic-pastoral hinterland. But the system of social stratification of the region displayed some ascriptive characteristics as will be seen.

VI

The general social structural setting of the section of Asia where untouchability has occurred has been described and related to our general theoretical views concerning social stratification. Now we can turn our attention to some of the specific combinations of events which within this area gave rise in some societies to a caste ethic with resultantly ritually differentiated social groups and in others to only the barest suggestion of these phenomena.

Regarding Japan, Korea and Tibet, the crucial variable seems to have been the entry of Mahayana Buddhism. Especially in Japan, where Shintoism had already set the stage for a caste ethic, the arrival of Mahayana in the seventh century A.D., with its aversion to violence toward living things and its elaborate doctrinal and organizational structure, brought about the crystalization of a morally intrinsic attitude toward occupations concerned with 'blood, death and dirt' and thereby played a role in bringing the Eta/Buraku into being. As for Korea, the Paekchong are to be found as a clearly untouchable category after the coming of Mahayana Buddhism in the sixth century A.D. Notes Passin.

> When Buddhism began to take hold in Korea...its proscription of the killing of animals and its vegetarianism played a very important role. The normal contempt for menial occupations was joined by the Buddhist judgment that they were not only contemptible but evil."[37]

The Ragyappa, by the very nature of one of their chief functions (breaking up corpses) presuppose the occurrence of Lamaistic Buddhism as a condition of their existence. They are defiled because their ritually essential task is profoundly abhorrent from the standpoint of the doctrine of *Ahimsa*. They are in this regard a typical social manifestation of the caste ethic.

In Southeast Asia, where civilization was less developed and later in coming, and where Hinayana Buddhism was initially the main religious diffusion, nothing resembling a caste system occurred aside from Bali. A caste ethic provoking abhorrence of lowly occupations and enjoining elaborate patterns of social avoidance and ritual purification in case of contact seems to have been absent. Only Bali displays castes at all on the Hindu model which seems in large part a result of the effects of Brahmanic penetration.[38] But even here, as noted above, the similarity is more apparent than real. We have noted that Burmese temple slaves were rated as pariahs at one time but this appears to be the only genuinely caste group the country has known and even this was not a permanent feature of the society.

Only in Ceylon, among the areas most heavily affected by Hinayana is there to be found a reasonably well-developed caste system. Yet even here the existence of outcaste groups is denied! However, it is clear that a caste ethic exists which, as Hocart puts it,[39] has made untouchability a fact of life, even though an officially unacknowledged one:

> I am not aware that at the present time any distinction is made in Ceylon between low castes and people outside (*sic*) the caste system, outcastes. Yet if the term does not exist, the institution does; the Rodiyas are completely outside the pale...they are completely excluded.[40]

In the ritual dimension of the Ceylonese caste system, barbers, drummers and potters perform roles involving contact with impure substances and for this reason bear to some degree the onus of a status which is not merely low but morally repellent. Respecting washermen, Hocart suggests that their "low rank" has "something to do with.. the washing away of menstrual blood."[41] In other words, in Ceylon, many occupations are regarded as a property of the persons performing them; occupational stratification is strongly ascription-oriented; hierarchical differences between occupational strata are regarded as being morally intrinsic.

Ceylon's caste ethic undoubtedly owes its emergence in some measure to the entry of Hinayana Buddhism. This commenced during the reign of Ashoka when, it is alleged,[42] this powerful ruler sent his son at the head of a missionary delegation to convert Ceylon to the "Dhamma". Whether specific qualities existed in pre-Mauryan Ceylonese society which predisposed it toward developing a stronger caste ethic than other areas affected by the Lesser Vehicle is difficult to say. One suspects that a most important consideration was Celyon's proximity to the Indian Subcontinent and the consequent facility with which people already steeped in the values of Indian social organization crossed over from the mainland.

In general, however, we have seen that the portions of Asia where the most clear-cut caste structures emerged were those which had developed the most complex nonindustrial societies and had received Mahayana Buddhism by diffusion later on—viz., North and Northeast Asia. The areas where the least clear-cut caste structures, or none at all, emerged were those which had developed smaller scale nonindustrial societies and had received, initially, primarily Hinayana Buddhism by diffusion—viz., Southeast Asia. Ceylon, on the other hand, is a special case, possibly arising from its contiguity to the mainland.

In both of its forms, then, Buddhism contained notions about existence and morality which when applied to the everyday affairs of men often tended to generate a caste ethic and invariably heightened awareness of pollution. So-called outcaste groups were especially likely to arise through the operation of this ethic because of Buddhism's strong preoccupation with the polluting implications of dirt, decay and death. Such preoccupations become readily understandable when we bear in mind that Buddhism in both its forms originated in India, the caste society *par excellence*.

We have already noted some of the events and conditions associated with the rise of Buddhism in India. Hinayana was the original form propounded by Buddha and his immediate followers. This was a comparatively simple moral-ethical system which eschewed many of the major doctrinal and ritual tenets of Hinduism. It was akin to later Buddhism in a manner not dissimilar to the relationship between "Nazarene" Christianity as propounded by the historical Christ and subsequent "Pauline"

Christianity which attained sufficient complexity and sophistication to permeate and ultimately outlive the Roman Empire.[43] But in either form, Buddhism was Indian, a product of men culturally rooted in the social structure and cultural life of India. Buddha was a Kshatriya, and as Crooke says:

> Buddha would undoubtedly have called himself a Hindu, and admitted that his was only one of the multitudinous sects which Hinduism is always throwing off...the movement was possibly as much social as theological. It found, on the one hand, a haughty, bigoted priesthood, on the other, an aristrocracy ruthless in its coercion of the lower races.[44]

The point is that ideas of purity and the abhorrence of killing, and a determination to translate these ideas into patterns of social avoidance and circumscription were not alien to Buddhism *in practice* but were on the contrary a rather natural part of its heritage. Ghurye is most explicit about this:

> ..according to later works dealing with Buddha's life, Buddha is never represented to have chosen any but the families of the two higher castes of his previous birth. In the opinion of the great majority of the monks, caste distinctions had value even after persons had joined the brotherhood...From these facts we conclude that in the matter of caste-restrictions the preachings and actions of Buddha had only a general liberalizing effect. He does not seem to have started with the idea of abolishing caste-distinctions, nor do his actions, as described in the Jataka stories, demonstrate an utter indifference towards the accident of birth; much less do they evince any conscious effort to annihilate caste.[45]

Within India, where a stronger caste ethic had been achieved under Hinduism, Buddhism in either of its forms was, in effect, a liberal doctrine in the sense that its moral tenets involved a more catholic approach to man. But Buddhism's greatest significance lay in its messianic activities outside India; and here, I contend, the moral implications of its doctrines resulted in the development of a caste ethic in certain other Asian

societies where heretofore such an ethic had either not existed or
had existed in a much weaker state of development. Put another
way, we might say that in India Buddhism was 'protestant' but
in the rest of Asia it was merely Indian.

Mahayana was especially influential in this respect because
it had reincorporated so much of the Hinduism which Hinayana
had rejected and because it developed an overall structure
(intellectual sophistication, large-scale monastic organization,
powerful synthesizing tendencies) which equipped it for the
task of penetrating the great nonindustrial societies north of
India. Mahayana achieved its definitive form in the crucible of
northwest India during the period when Hellenism, Buddhism
and Chinese Civilization were converging there. This is the so-
called Kushana Period when, as Rawlinson declares, "Buddhism
...was transformed from a highly individualistic philosophy
of life into a world religion, and spread along the Central Asian
trade routes...to China itself."[16]

Yet China herself did not really develop castes and/or outcaste groups in the full sense of the word. She did not go much
beyond the normal amount of status rigidity characteristic of
ascription-oriented societies. Many of the preconditions which
in Korea and Japan conduced to a caste ethic existed there, but,
as noted earlier, China's Confucian ethic, with its acceptance of
certain achievement-oriented principles, might have worked at
opposite purposes to the former. Or this is what I would hypo-
thesize. There is also another factor which may have been just
as important in preventing Buddhism from gaining the kind of
hold on Chinese society necessary to promote a caste ethic. One
might call this the failure of Chinese Buddhism to rise above
'politics' and achieve a position of absolute sacrosanctity. This
in turn might have been a function of China's imperial structure
which made the emperor's status and virtue dependent upon his
ability to maintain order and prosperity; for when a dynasty
was discredited, usually the groups and ideas it supported were
discredited along with it. Put differently, it might be suggested
that the bifurcation of priestly and kingly functions and their
consequent assignment to two morally differentiated strata (the
Brahman and Kshatriya *Varnas*) in India effectively removed
the moral order from any danger of being implicated in the
political misfortunes of mundane dynasties. Because this bifurc-

ation did not occur in China, the fortunes of the religious system were frequently tied to the fortunes of the political order.

Space does not permit a long discussion of this point, but perhaps the rough lineaments of the argument can be traced. Mahayana Buddhism began making serious inroads into China during the second century A.D., as the second Han Dynasty was in the process of a devastating collapse. A passage from Arthur F. Wright's matchless essay on the "interaction" of Buddhism and Chinese society describes the setting:

> ...the upper level of the Han sociopolitical order was riven by conflict...the moral and political sanctions of an earlier day were undermined and discredited...a mood of uncertainty and questioning developed within the elite.
> Upon the peasantry fell the burden of supporting a corrupt and divided upper class.. In the years before 317, therefore, the peasantry is sunk in misery and sullen discontent ...the breakup of the Han peasant society, then, is one of the factors that prepared the way in this period for the spread of an alien religion.[47]

For a time, according to Wright, Taoism filled part of this gulf, but ultimately it was Buddhism which took over the major role as a "protestant" doctrine to which the elite could turn intellectually and the masses could turn ritualistically. Buddhism grew in importance throughout the period of chaos which followed the Han's disintegration and reached its climax during the next period of dynastic florescence, the Sui-T'ang (Sui unification of the north occurred from 581-589). But even at its florescence Buddhism never succeeded in dissociating itself from the dynasties which officially supported it. Thus, when the T'ang emperors began declining in esteem due to a waning of their imperial fortunes, a resurgence of Confucianism occurred which grew to such an extent that by the ninth century, Buddhism was experiencing persecution. After 900, the Buddhism that remained was far short of the universalistic moral position it had come to enjoy in so many other parts of Asia and which Hinduism had long enjoyed in India. Chinese Civilization had incorporated some Buddhist tenets into its dominantly Confucian and Taoist syntheses, but had left the "ecclesiastical structure" subject to mundane fortune. From China, however, Mahayana diffused to Korea and Japan and there had come to enjoy a much more commanding moral position.

Yet Buddhism was not entirely without its effects upon Chinese society. During the Sui-T'ang, Buddhism's ethical rejection of killing was reflected in certain state policies:

> The suspension of state business was decreed for certain of the Buddhist holy days, and the state ordered the cessation of all executions, killing and butchering during the days of special observances in the three months of Buddhist abstinence.
> The severity of the penal code was somewhat moderated, and the death penalty was used more sparingly.[48]

Moreover, by the time of Buddhism's advent in China, a category of occupational roles had come to be adjudged so abominable that their practitioners were declared ineligible to take the Confucian civil service examinations. These were the so-called "Mean People" who, according to Chang,[49] included policemen, lictors, jailers, gatekeepers, coroners, grain collectors and runners. Chang's list refers to a comparatively late period in Chinese history (the Ch'ing Dynasty), long after Buddhism's heyday had passed. One can only wonder whether such roles as butchering, barbering, tanning and scavenging were ever morally interdicted in earlier times. Personally, I suspect not, at least not to the same degree as after the advent of Buddhism. As was the case in Japan, it seems reasonable to conclude that Buddhism might have helped in some measure to intensify the judgment that certain 'dirty' occupations were sufficiently morally repugnant to warrant singling out their practitioners for a special measure of social denigration. It seems equally plausible that Buddhism was instrumental in defining certain occupations as polluting which had not been previously so regarded.

VII

We can but briefly allude to other parts of the world where some sort of caste ethic has arisen. In Polynesia, tribal life grew sufficiently complex to give rise to some measure of stratification.[50] Nobles and commoners were subdivided on the basis of a concept of *mana*. Royal personages could not be approached by the laity without this incurring dreadful magical consequences. In West Africa, kings were often held to be morally sacrosanct while iron workers, on the other hand, were considered polluted and subject to avoidance. Colonialism, since it involves unequal relationships between people of different ethnic and technological antecedents, has shown a capacity to generate a kind of caste ethic. Modern racism is one of its chief sociological by-products. In both South Africa and America this has led to the systems of Apartheid and Segregation, respectively, where whites interdict marriages and other forms of social relationships between themselves and Blacks on the grounds that the latter possess biologically heritable inferior traits.

Greece and Rome, and Medieval Europe, require a brief comment. In the Graeco-Roman world there was a distinction between freemen ('citizens') and slaves ('non-citizens') which had some caste overtones; but the possibility of legally transforming oneself from the latter to the former status naturally mitigated the effect of the distinction to some degree. Church Universalism during the Middle Ages had a similar effect, although the social order was rigidly ascription-oriented and some of the 'dirty' occupations carried the aura of moral repugnance. But it cannot be said that a caste system existed in which groups of functionally essential occupations were placed morally outside the pale.

The point that stands out when we consider caste-type social stratification outside the orbit of "Pan-Indian Civilization", to use Leach's phrase,[51] is that occupations are not necessarily the basis of distinctions to which a concept of pollution or moral inferiority is applied. In racist social stratification systems the concept is applied to alleged biological differences. In what Nadel calls "conquest states" such as are found in parts of Africa, ethnic, political and military considerations combine to determine the criteria for arranging groups in hierarchical layers and assigning them differential functions and worth.[52] Even the "mystic duties" of different clans, rather than 'occupations' in the strict sense of the word, may become the basis of such organization. Says Nadel of the Nuba Clans:

> There is no differentiation in ordinary occupation, all being farmers and owners of livestock. But there is an important differentiation in ritual rights and obligations. For each clan is believed to possess certain supernatural powers peculiar to it and to no other clan, which enable it to control a part of the universe . not only for its own benefit but...on behalf of the tribe at large, so that, together, the clans ensure—in a supernatural sense—the survival of the tribe and safeguard its welfare.[53]

Two clans even qualify as "untouchable," it would seem, inasmuch as their "mystic duties" cause them to be avoided out of fear of what the misdirection of their supernatural powers might lead to.

Enough has been said here, it is hoped, to suggest both the complexity and the fascination of the problem of comparative social stratification and within it the genesis and nature of caste organization. This essay has been mainly an attempt to outline what I believe to be a possible analytical approach to the matter. Primarily, it seems to me, the problem is one of carefully defining terms, separating variables and then establishing the relationships among these variables.

NOTES AND REFERENCES

[1] *The Report of the Commissioner for Scheduled Castes and Scheduled Tribes* (1955-56) reveals that Untouchables number 55, 327, 021 and that Scheduled Tribes number an additional 22, 511, 857. This yields a total of 77, 838, 878 who are heavily defiled from an orthodox Hindu standpoint

[2] On the Eta see Donoghue (1957), Ninomiya (1933), Cornell (1967); on the Paekchong see Osgood (1951); on the Ragyappa see Bell (1924, 1928).

[3] On Ceylon see Hocart (1950), Yalman (1960).

[4] On Burma see Hutton (1946); on China see Chang (1955).

[5] On Polynesia see Hocart (1950); on the South see Dumont (1961), Dollard (1949).

[6] Readers of the original version of this paper (Gould, 1960) will

recognize that considerable revision has been undertaken in many places. This version still falls far short of correcting all the deficiencies which I know my arguments contain and which in time I hope can be more fully rectified.

[7] As Tumin (1952: 3), among many others, has pointed out.

[8] The term 'work' is meant here in the broad sense of any full-time specialization.

[9] Figures supplied by the U. S. Government in the *Dictionary of Occupational Titles* show that in an industrial society like the U.S.A. in the sixties there are more than 20,000 identifiable occupations.

[10] My thinking in this portion of the essay have been considerably influenced by Homans' (1949) book, *The Human Group*, and by the writings of Parsons (1953) and his collaborators.

[11] A most important discussion of the structural foundations of the relationship between social organization and caste functions is Levi-Strauss (1963).

[12] China was one limited exception, as we shall see below. Many nonindustrial societies which tended to identify persons with occupational role, but which did not develop a strong caste ethic, afforded some latitude for social mobility either through hypergamy or through simple change of occupation. Egypt, according to Ghurye (1957), went through different phases on this score at different points in her history. During the "Pyramidic Age," although there was ascription-orientation respecting most categories of work, "the...professions...of a priest, a scribe, and a warrior, though generally they are in the same families, yet there was no restriction against anyone following any of these callings, even if one's father might not have professed that particular calling but had carried on one of the other two." (p. 144) Things changed by the early Ptolemies. By then, "only persons descended from a priest could enter their profession." (p. 144).

[13] See Gould (1959, 1963, 1964, 1965), Bennett and Despres (1959), Pocock (1962).

[14] See Tax (1953).

[15] See Redfield (1957).

[16] The term is useful to dramatize the striking nature of such groups, but from a theoretical standpoint it is highly misleading.

[17] See Gould (1958).

[18] Since originally writing this essay, much more evidence in support of this statement has been found. In later publications it will be presented.

[19] See his *Caste, Class and Race in India*, 1957.

[20] In Africa, where inter-tribal accommodations took place in the context of lower technological levels, the resultant 'caste system' was far less elaborate than in India where both ethnic and technological complexity were far greater.

[21] My use of the word 'difference' here is intended to convey a notion which Pocock (1957) has elaborated.

[22]"Untouchability in the Far East", p. 40.
[23]Ibid.
[24]In *Caste in India*, 1951.
[25]See Wheeler (1953) and Piggott (1950).
[26]Linton (1954).
[27]Hutton (1951), Ghurye (1957).
[28]See Davids (1903). Ghurye (1957).
[29]Davids (1903). Italics are mine.
[30]See Rawlinson (1953).
[31]See Linton (1954), Childe (1941, 1946).
[32]See Goodrich (1951), Chang (1955).
[33]Sansom (1955).
[34]Ibid., p. 37.
[35]Linton (1954).
[36]See Shen and Liu (1953).
[37]Ibid., p. 37.
[38]See Linton (1954).
[39]In *Caste*, 1950.
[40]Ibid., p. 6.
[41]Ibid.
[42]See Smith (1958).
[42]See Gibbon (1941).
[44]*The Northwestern Provinces of India*, 1879, p. 67.
[45]Ibid., pp. 71-72. I think that what we have failed to make sufficiently clear in evaluating the sociological consequences of Buddhism, is the fact that the relaxation of caste rules, to the extent that there was such a relaxation at all, was promulgated primarily *within* the *sanghas* but not in society as a whole. Buddhism's ethical criticism of society took the form of inducing its followers to renounce the lay society of caste differentiation and preoccupation with mundane pursuits and opt for the *sanghas* where there things were subordinated to the collective search for salvation. Such an ethical orientation to the 'sins of the world' would accord perfectly with the renunciatory orientation of all Indian religions—*viz.*, you 'cure' the evil in the world by renouncing the world, not by reforming it. In this sense, the relatively equalitarian *sanghas* must have been conceived as earthly way-stations on the pathway to Nirvana.
[46]Ibid., p. 79.
[47]See Wright (1957).
[48]Ibid., p. 32.
[49]*The Chinese Gentry*, 1955
[50]Hocart, 1950.
[51]"Introduction" to *Aspects of Caste in South India, Ceylon and North-West Pakistan*, 1960.
[52]"Caste and Government in Primitive Society," 1954. Page numbers are not given because I have used a typescript copy of the article and do not have the original available.
[53]Ibid.

BIBLIOGRAPHY

Bell, C., *Tibet, Past and Present.* London: Oxford Clarendon Press, 1924.
——, *The People of Tibet.* London: Oxford Clarendon Press, 1928.
Bennett, John W. and Leo Despress, "Kinship and Instrumental Activities: A Theoretical Inquiry," *American Anthropologist,* 62: 254-67, 1960.
Berreman, Gerald D., "Caste in India and the United States, *"The American Journal of Sociology* Vol. 66: 120-127, 1960.
Chang, Chung-li, *The Chinese Gentry.* Seattle: University of Washington Press, 1955.
Childe, V. Gordon, *Man Makes Himself.* New York: Mentor Books, 1941.
——, *What Happened in History.* London: Penguin Books. 1946.
Cornell, John B., "From Caste Patron to Entrepreneur and Political Ideologue: Transformation in 19th and 20th Century Outcaste Leadership Elites," in Bernard S. Silberman and Harry D. Hartoonian, Editors, *Modren Japanese Leadership: Transition and Change.* Tucson, Arizona: University of Arizona Press: 51-81, 1966.
Crooke, William, *The Northwestern Provinces of India.* London: Methuen, 1879.
Davids, Rhys, *Buddhist India.* Calcutta: Susil Gupta, 1903.
Dollard, John, *Caste and Class in a Southern Town.* New York: Harper & Co., 1949.
Donaghue, John, "An Eta Community in Japan: The Social Persistence of Outcaste Groups," *American Anthropologist* 59, No. 6: 1000-1017, 1957.
Dumont, Louis, "Caste, Racism and 'Stratification ?" *Contributions to Indian Sociology,* No. V: 20-43, The Hague: Mouton & Co , 1961.
Fortes, Meyer, Ed., *African Political Sys.ems.* London: Oxford University Press, 1950,
Ghurye, G. S., *Caste, Class and Race in India.* Bombay: Popular Book Depot, 1957.
Gibbon, Edmund, *The Decline and Fall of the Roman Empire.* New York: Modern Library. 2 vols., 1941.
Goodrich, L. Carrington, A Short History of the Chinese People. New York: 1951.
Gould, Harold A., "The Hindu Jajmani System: A Case of Economic Particularism," *Southwestern Journal of Anthropology* 14; No. 4: 428-437, 1958. Also Chapter 5 in this volume.
——, "The Peasant Village: Centrifugal or Centripetal ?" *Eastern Anthropologist,* 13: 1-16, 1959.
——, "Lucknow Rickshawallas: The Social Organization an Occupational Category," *International Journal •of Comparative Sociology* IV: 24-47, 1965.
Hocart, A. M., *Caste.* London: Methuen, 1950.
Homans, George C., *The Human Group.* London: Routledge, 1949.
Leach, Edmund, "Introduction: What Should We Mean By Caste?" In

Edmund Leach, Editor, *Aspects of Caste in South India, Ceylon and North-West Pakistan.* Cambridge Papers in Social Anthropology. London: Cambridge University Press: 1-10, 1960.

Levi-Strauss, Claude, "The Bear and the Barber," *Journal of the Royal Anthropological Institute* 93: 1-11, 1963.

Linton. Ralph, *The Tree of Culture* New York: Alfred A. Knopf, 1954.

Nadel, S. F., "Caste and Government in Primitive Society," *The Journal of The Anthropological Society of Bombay* 8: 9-22, 1954.

Ninomiya, S., "An Inquiry Concerning the Origin, Development, and Present Situation of the Eta in Relation to the History of Social Classes in Japan," *Transactions of the Asiatic Society of Japan,* Series 2, Volume 10, 1933.

Osgood, C., *The Koreans and their Culture* New York: Ronald Press, 1951.

Parsons, Talcott, Edward Shils, et. al., *Toward a General Theory of Action.* Cambridge, Mass.: Harvard University Press,- 1953.

Passin, Herbert, Untouchability in the Far East," *Monuments Niponica* XI: 27-47, 1955.

Piggott, Stuart, *Prehistoric India.* London: Penguin Books, 1950.

Pocock, David F., "Inclusion and Exclusion: A Process in the Caste System of Gujerat, "*Southwestern Journal of Anthropology* 13: 19-31, 1957.

———, "Difference' in East Africa: A Study of Caste and Religion in Modern Indian Society," *Southwestern Journal of Anthropology* 13: 289-300, 1957.

———, "Notes on *Jajmani* Relationships," *Contributions to Indian Sociology,* No. VI; 78-95, The Hague: Mouton & Co., 1962.

Rawlinson, H. G., *India, A Cultural History.* New York: Praeger, 1953.

Redfield, Robert, *The Folk Culture of Yucatan.* Chicago: University Press, 1953.

Sansom, George B., *A Short History of Japan.* New York: Appleton, Century, Crofts, 1955.

Shen, Tsung-Lien and Shen-Chi Liu, *Tibet and the Tibetans,* Stanford: Stanford University Press, 1953.

Smith, Vincent, A., *The Oxford History of India,* London: Oxford University Press, 1958.

Tax, Sol, *Penny Capitalism in a Guatemalan Community.* Washington: Smithsonian Inst', 1953.

Tumin, Melvin, Caste in Latin America. Princeton, N.J.: Princeton University Press, 1952.

Wheeler, Sir Mortimer, *The Indus Valley Civilization.* Cambridge: Cambridge University Press, 1953.

Wright, Arthur F., "Buddhism and Chinese Culture: Phases of Interaction," *Journal of Asian Studies,* XVII, No. 1: 17-42, 1957.

Yalman, Nur, "The Flexibility of Caste Principles in a Kandyan Community," in Edmund Leach, Editor, *Aspects of Caste in South India, Ceylon and North-West Pakistan.* Cambridge Papers in Social Anthropology, Cambridge University Press: 78-112, 1960.

4

Priest and Contrapriest: A Structural Analysis of Jajmani Relationship in the Hindu Plains and the Nilgiri Hills

I

In a thoughtful essay published several years ago a strong case was made for a 'Sociology of India' (Dumont and Pocock 1957)

Such an approach, it was asserted, "lies at the confluence of Sociology and Indology." Its value stems from the recognition that 'India is *one*"; that the "traditional, sanskritic civilization demonstrates without question the unity of India." (p. 9) Once this essential unity is recognized and becomes itself a datum of our sociological analysis, we move rapidly "from haphazard notes to exhaustive, intensive study, and from isolated features to sets of relations between features." Henceforth, "the empirical diversity recedes to the background, and an almost monotonous similarity springs forth." (p. 10)

What follows is essentially an affirmation of the view that there is a 'Sociology of India' and that the marriage of Indology and Sociology does indeed provide a means of revealing certain constancies at the level of 'relations between features' (in this instance, with respect to traditional economic interaction) which impose order on what otherwise might seem to be a heterogeneity of disparate items of behavior. Even more, it will be shown that knowledge of the 'fundamental unexpressed ideas' underlying Hindu Civilization (identifiable through the study of Indology and through the scientific observation of contemporary India) allows us to comprehend institutions which are the result of the diffusion of such fundamental ideas to regions beyond the main stream of Hindu Civilization. It is in this latter connection that we shall consider the system of ritualized economic interaction found among the tribes of the Nilgiri Hills in South India.

II

As we proceed with this essay it will become increasingly evident that we are dealing to a very high degree with the connections existing between ways of *thinking* about social relationships and the corresponding ways in which the relationships themselves are articulated in the domain of concrete behavior. It will become equally evident that both thought and social relationships are held to be interconnected phenomena within a socio-cultural field which comprises a whole— the whole in this instance being Indian society. These are obviously not original realizations; they are the heritage of Emile Durkheim and his French school of Sociology which culminate today in the scholarship of Professor Claude Levi Strauss.

Durkheim saw that social phenomena and individual psychological phenomena constitute two levels or orders of 'reality' for each of which a distinct set of 'facts' and a distinct set of analytical procedures are appropriate. Society consists of aggregates of beings whose relationships with one another are *as aggregates*; it is the nature of and interrelationships among these aggregates which constitutes the subjectmatter of a genuine sociological analysis. In modern anthropological parlance, the study of the 'laws of aggregation' is simply the study of social structure in the broad sense. What interested Durkheim were the intrinsic properties of social systems, the properties which differentiate them internally and from each other. In social differentiation, Durkheim saw the ultimate basis of social solidarity. The social whole is divided into interdependent parts each of which contributes something to its overall nature and makes it more than the mere sum of its constituent parts

However, Durkheim's view of unity through interdependence led him to the concept of *opposition* rather than to a simple notion of harmonious, pristine functional interrelationships. That is, social integration was seen to arise from a process of *absolute* demarcation of one social domain from another. Respecting religion, he declared:

> All known religious beliefs, whether simple or complex, present one common characteristic: they presuppose a classification of all things, real and ideal, of which men think, into two classes or opposed groups, generally designated by two distinct terms which are translated well enough by the words profane and sacred. This division of the world into two domains, the one containing all that is sacred, the other all that is profane, is the distinctive trait of religious thought . . . (Durkheim 1947: 37)

He goes on to say (Durkheim 1947: 39-40) that this opposition 'frequently degenerates (*sic*) into a veritable antagonism.' And, he continues:

> The two worlds are not only conceived of as separate, but as even hostile and jealous rivals of each other. Since man cannot fully belong to one except on condition of leaving the other completely, they are exhorted to withdraw themselves completely from the profane world, in order to lead an exclusively religious life. Hence comes . . . monasticism . . .

At the root of this perception of a kind of antagonism between the structural components of society, I feel, was a dawning quest for a deeper understanding of the relationship between mind and the social milieu. It expressed itself in rather crude characterizations of a kind of war between social institutions because Durkheim was himself groping for an intellectual framework capable of concretizing his real concerns. Statements in the foregoing passages, such as that religious beliefs 'presuppose a classification' of things into 'two classes' or (reductionistically) 'two groups', bespeak his halting efforts to express what he means. Passages in other parts of *Les Formes Elementaires* much more clearly reveal the direction in which Durkheim was trying to move. He declares that religious beliefs 'presuppose a classification' which is the product of *thought* ('of which men think,). Elsewhere he says that the phenomena subsumed under *sacred* and *profane* represent a 'classification of things.' (1947: 38) In the end, however, and quite understandably, Durkheim could not quite rise above the intellectual conventions of his day. For that reason, he continued to think reductionistically and believe that the roots of classification lay primarily in the structure of society itself. Society is 'a whole', said he,

> ... or rather it is *the* unique whole to which everything is related. Thus logical hierarchy is only another aspect of social hierarchy; and the unity of knowledge is nothing else than the very unity of the collectivity; extended to the universe.

Durkheim, in other words, succeeded in emancipating sociology from the quick-sand of psychological reductionism, only to deliver it into the equally treacherous hands of sociological reductionism. In the process, however, he made major new contributions to thinking on the subject of the relationship between mind and society which subsequent scholars have carried forward. This has been especially the contribution of Professor Claude Levi-Strauss and, in general, the field of structural anthropology.

The realization that the structure of mind and the structure of society are not simply projections of the one into the other, *in either direction*, is cogently expressed by Professor Levi-Strauss in *Totemism* (1962: 90). The "laws of association" it is stated, are not compehended by the assumption that mind is "an inert product of the action of the environment on an amorphous unconsciousness"; rather they are comprehended by the realization that consciousness arises out of the capacity of mind to be itself an active agent. Consciousness displays 'an original logic', a direct expression of the structure of the mind (and behind mind, probably of the brain). This is "the logic of oppositions and correlations, exclusions and inclusions, compatibilities and incompatibilities." (*Totemism* 1962: 90) Thus Durkheim's posited opposition between sacred and profane, by which religion is demarcated from the rest of society, and behaviour appropriate to each sphere is classified, is shown by Professor Levi-Strauss to be compatible with the manner in which the mind, as it were, 'thinks demarcatevely'.

This is not to say, of course, that mind is independent of the social milieu or that mind *causes* the social milieu. This is no more the case than is the original Durkheimian notion that social structure is merely the basis for the categories employed by mind. What is being said is that the relationship between *thinking* (i. e. logic, conceptualization) and social processes is extremely subtle and not one-to-one. It is a matter, perhaps we can say, of a complex interaction and interrelationship between 'levels of mind' and 'levels of social action, As Levi-Strauss puts it:

> Each level of social reality appears . . . as an indispensable complement, without which it would be impossible to understand the other levels. Customs lead to beliefs, and these lead to techniques, but the different levels do not simply reflect each other. They react dialectically among themselves in such a way that we cannot hope to understand one of them without first evalutating, through their respective relations of opposition and correlation, *institutions, representations*, and *situations*. In every one of its practical undertakings, anthropology thus does no more than assert a *homology of structure* between human thought and the human object to which it is applied. (1962: 91)

In the application of this methodology to totemism, caste and myth, Professor Levi-Strauss argues that the role played by these phenomena in *social reality* is missed if their referents (animals, 'barbers', and demi-beings) are interpreted as possessing *intrinsic* importance to people. As he puts it, with reference to the evolution of Radcliffe-Brown's anthropology (1963: 2), "in 1929, Radcliffe-Brown believed that interest was conferred upon animals and plants because they were 'eatable', in 1951 he saw clearly that the real reason for their interest lay in the fact that they are, if I may use a word, "thinkable". With reference to totemism, Levi-Strauss continues (1963: 2) :

> Therefore totemic ideas appear to provide a *code enabling man to express isomorphic properties between nature and culture*. Obviously, there exists here some kind of similarity with linguistics, since language is also a code which through oppositions between difference, permits us to convey meanings. (Italics are mine)

In both cases, selection is made from "the complete series of empirical media" (in languages "vocal articulation"; in totemism: "the entire wealth of the biological world") of a few elements which "can be organized in strongly and unequivocally contrasting pairs." The purpose of such selection does not lie, "as the functionalist school assumes, in the utilitarian properties of biological species as mankind conceives them, but rather in their logical properties, that is, their ability to serve as symbols expressing contrasts and oppositions." (1963: 2)

III

Work presented by Orenstein (1965a, 1965b) affords us an excellent platform from which the insights of Durkheim, Levi-Strauss and the structural school can be carried effectively into the domain of Indian sociology and applied to a specific institutional area. Orenstein has examined Hindu caste values from the standpoint of their constituting a "code", a "non-linguitsic normative system", which has been built up out of "the assumptions that their bearers hold about the world." These assumptions, he contends, are what Professor Levi-Strauss calls the "unconscious infrastructure" of a culture. I propose now to elucidate Professor Orenstein's 'structural analysis' of Hindu caste values in order to lay down a basis for showing how these values and the 'unconscious infrastructure' underlying them makes comprehensible ritualized economic interaction (the *jajmani* system) not only in the Plains of Hindustan but in the Nilgiri Hills as well.

What Schweitzer (1957) terms 'world and life negation' clearly arises from one of the most fundamental assumptions which Hindus make about the world. But this negative evaluation of the world was not as all-encompassing as Schweitzer implies in his endeavour to sharpen a contrast he was trying to draw between the predominant moral-ethical orientation of India and the Judeo-Christian West. As Orenstein emphasizes (1965a.: 10 11), "pollution was conceived by the law givers primarily in biological terms." That is, from the range of posssible perceptions of relations between things in nature, a distinction was drawn between a corporeal, transient (finite in time) aspect of life and a contrasting 'essence' which was somehow eternal and unchanging because non-corporeal and non-transient. This, I think, comes out vividly in Upanishadic thought where the nature of this 'essence' is almost always stated in negative phraseology—that is, it is depicted as that which the corporeal, the transient, the biological *is not*. Thus (Hume 1934):

Not by speech, not by mind,
Not by sight can He be comprehended.
How can He be comprehended
Otherwise than by one's saying 'He is.!'? (*Katha* 6:12)

Opposition between sacred and profane is, then, coded as an opposition between *pollution* ('involvement with life substance and process') and *purity* ('the absence of biological involvement'). The qualities associated with each domain are then elaborated, as are the modes of behavior appropriate to each and the means of making transitions from the one to the other.

Another fundamental assumption which Hindus make about the world is 'hierarchy'. (*cf.* Bougle 1958; Dumont and Pocock 1958; and Pocock 1957). This was coded into their value systems along with the purity/pollution opposition. Essentially, hierarchy can be seen logically as a means of applying the notion of opposition vertically and serially. Where could this concept have come from? Quite plausibly from the observation of and. as Swanson (1960) has suggested, reflection upon society itself, which as a form in nature predates man himself by millions of years.

We must bear in mind that Hinduism and Indian Civilization arose in the context of a complex technology and an urban society that was highly elaborated occupationally and socially stratified. Elaborate hierarchy was, and is, an implicit feature of all stratified societies. Swanson (1960) has sought to demonstrate that, underlyingly, models of religious systems are homologous with (though not reducible to) the structure of the social wholes containing them.

Another underlying assumption of Hinduism which is visible in caste is what I have called (Chapter 2) 'ascription-orientation'. By this is meant the tendency to regard the occupational role and the role-occupant as being identical. This is a datum of experience natural to preindustrial urban societies by contrast with industrial societies. The nature of technology and concomitant, supportive social structures in the preindustrial urban societies is responsible for this. Work is specialized in such societies; there are artisans, peasants, soldiers, menials, priests, rulers, scholars, etc. But specialized work nevertheless tends to be situated in kin groups which are in turn situated in small communities; most are in villages, the remainder in towns and comparatively small cities. Work is rarely situated in bureaucratic groups, as is the case with most work performed in industrial societies, where personalistic ties are secondary and social relationships relative to work contexts are predominantly impersonal. Work roles in the preindustrial societies are therefore normally seen as mere aspects of the inheritance of property through the system of descent. They are, to put it simply, regarded as being hereditary, part of that which is acquired through biological process.

Among a people, then, where collective experience has generated the assumption that biological process connotes *pollution* and its absence connotes *purity*, where relations between objects are perceived in hierarchical terms, and where the technological integration characteristic of preindustrial urban societies predisposes people toward perceiving occupations as being implicated in biological process, it is not surprising to learn that the division of labour and its economic ramifications are subject to the jurisdiction of "the sacred laws of Hinduism, or Dharmashastra." Let us try to summarize these underlying assumptions out of which Hindu sacred law seems to have been coded :

1. There is a domain of the *sacred* and a domain of the *profane* which are absolutely opposed to one another.
2. *Purity* and *pollution* are the intrinsic qualities of the *sacred* and the *profane* respectively.
3. Life substance and process (corporeal, transient) signify *pollution*; the opposite of life substance and process (incorporeal, non-transient 'essence') signify *purity*.
4. Work (in the 'ascription-oriented' complex society) is inherited through the same biological process by which all aspects of life-substance are acquired and is therefore subject to the same cannons of valuation as all other aspects of life-substance.
5. The differences between objects engendered by biological process are ordered hierarchically.
6. Position in hierarchy signifies degree of *purity/sacredness/* 'involvement in life-process': The higher an object is, valuationally, the more *pure/sacred/*'uninvolved in life process'; the lower the object, the more *impure/profane/* 'involved in life process.'

A final observation must be made concerning the precise nature of pollution as seen by the Hindu. Clearly, it is not so much biological process *per se* that is perceived as the source of pollution as it is those aspects of the process which involve death, decay, waste, and evil. Orenstein (1965b: 1) quotes Vishnu XXXV (xcvi: 43-40) as saying that the body is a "receptacle of impure substance," which is constantly subject to destruction, "the stay of carnal desire, wrath, greed." Through this 'logic' arises the hierarchical division of society in the *Varnas*: the most polluted *Varna* the Sudra, consists of the *jatis* whose *ascribed* (i. e. biologically inherited) work in economic society and in rituals means involvement with decay, death, waste and (by implication) evil. For this reason, Passin's (1955) statement that untouchability applies to groups whose work puts them in contact with 'blood, death and dirt' appears to be both an accurate and a succinct way of summarizing this feature of caste organization.

Let us next turn to the operation of these assumptions in the coding of Hindu Sacred Law and see how the resultant code makes possible the 'logical' derivation of the caste and *jajmani* systems in Hindu India and the system of ritualized economic interaction found in the Nilgiri Hills of South India. As Orenstein rightly expresses it, we are dealing with a kind of 'grammar' the learning of which enables one to 'speak' the 'language' of Hindu social organization. In my discussion of caste, I shall simply present Orenstein's position, interspersed with personal comments, since my purpose henceforth will be to use the discussion of caste only as the necessary point of departure for dealing with Hindu and Nilgiri economic interaction.

Orenstein believes that the Dharmashastras deal with two fundamental types of pollution. He calls these, after his 'linguistic model', *intransitive* and *transitive* pollution. "Each of these types of pollution," he declares (1965b: 2), "is associated with distinctive 'paradigms', by which I mean orderly variations on rules not unlike the declensions of grammar." In his own words :

(1) When a birth or death occurs in Ego's kin group he is subject to *intransitive pollution* . . . Defilement is believed to 'spread' through the kin group, which is conceived . . . as 'connected by particles of the same body.' As in the grammatical intransitive, there is no object of action. (1965b: 2) . . . *The extent of intransitive pollution . . . is proportionate to varna rank, i.e,, the higher the rank the less the pollution* . . . each *varna*, including the Brahman, was conceived as having associated with it a 'normal' amount of pollution paralleling its rank. The lower *varnas*, in other words, were assumed to be naturally and normally more deeply implicated with life substance and process than the higher ones. (1965a: 10-11)

(2) *Transitive pollution* is incurred through interaction with biological phenomena. It is subdivided into (a) *internal pollution*, in which Ego, as subject, acts upon objects, and (b) *external pollution*, in which Ego is the object . . . External pollution is brought on if one

contacts biological substance or process, for example
by touching or eating dead matter or bodily secretions.
(1965b: 2) ... *The* extent of *transitive pollution*... *is
proportionate to varna rank. 2a) The extent of internal pollution is proportionate to the purity of the varna
harmed. 2b) The extent of the external pollution is
proportionate to the defilement of the varna contacted.*
(1965a: 10)

Hierarchical or *varna* status is, then, determined by the
degree of normal purity which a *varna* enjoys. The higher the
varna the greater the amount of intransitive pollution that
occurs whenever this state of normal purity is disturbed by
birth, death, and other 'dangerous' events. A fundamental
criterion of the degree of this normal purity (*varna status*) is the
extent to which a given *jati* (the widest extension of the notion
of 'common body particles') performs or avoids hereditary work
associated with 'blood, death and dirt'. The higher the *varna* of
a *jati* the nearer it is to identity with the *sacred* (non-involvement with biological process), the lower it is the more it is
identified with the *profane* (involvement with biological process).
Society (*varna/jati*) is thus a series of oppositions between pure
(*sacred*) and impure (*profane*) arranged in vertical (hierarchical)
order embracing corporeal man: Brahman vs Kshatriya,
Sudra ·]/Kshatriya vs Vaisya, Twice Born vs Once Born,
Touchable vs Untouchable.

As hierarchical, or *varna*, status is dependent on the degree
of normal purity enjoyed, so also it is dependent on the extent
to which impurity can be avoided. That is, it is also dependent
on success in dealing with transitive pollution—the avoidance of
contact with polluted objects (internal) and the avoidance of
being contacted by polluting objects (external). The more impurity can be transferred to others, and the more others can be
prevented from transmitting impurity to oneself, the greater is
one's proximity to the *sacred* (pure), and vice versa. However,
the greater the success in avoiding pollution, the greater the
danger which pollution presents.

The Brahman *varna* is the highest, purest and most sacred
because it is the repository of the Sacred Knowledge and is, in
the traditional occupations practiced by its *jatis*, the social

embodiment of the injunction to avoid involvement in biological process. The Kshatriya is the next highest *varna* because while its *jatis* traditionally perform the tasks of political and military leadership, the governing of men demands at times the spilling of blood. A revealing passage from Gautama, cited by Orenstein (1965 b : 7), vividly expresses this: "Gautama also relieves monarchs of the burden of impurity 'lest their business be impeded.' (Buhler 1879 : 251)". Dumont (1962 : 51) makes the same observation but stresses the interdependence of Brahman and Kshatriya *varnas*. Says he :

> Concretely, the relation between the functions of priest and king has a double aspect. While spiritually, absolutely, the priest is superior he is at the same time, from a temporal or material point of view, subject and dependent. And conversely the king, if spiritually subordinate, is materially the master.

Thus :

> It is not enough that the king should employ Brahmans for the public ritual, he must also have a permanent, personal relationship with one particular Brahman, his *purohita*, literally 'the one placed in front' ... The gods do not eat the offerings of a king devoid of *purohita* ... the king depends on him for all the actions of his life, for these would not succeed without him.

Jatis included in the Vaisya *varna* seem to comprise a residuum consisting of those whose occupations afford them too little natural purity to be higher in rank but too much to warrant their relegation to Once Born or Sudra status. The Sudra *varna*, on the other hand, is identified with *jatis* whose occupations involve the deepest immersion in, and therefore the closest contact with, biological process ('Blood, death and dirt'). They possess, as it were, little or no natural purity.

One of the chief ways in which the caste system enunciates the 'grammar' of Hindu sacred law is in the domain of economic interaction, for in a real sense it is possible to contend that participants in such a system are ultimately engaged in the perpetual exchange of two properties—*viz.*, 'purity' and 'commodities' (primarily *grain*, or things which stand for it). These exchanges occur along two continua and proceed according to rules which reflect the assumptions about the cosmos and nature which came into being with the dawning of Indian Civilization, a particular selection and integration of the phenomena of human experience. One continuum concerns the performance of ritual services; the other concerns the performance of economic services *per se*.

In the ritual continuum, two interrelated processes of exchange are involved. These processes arise from the nature of Hindu ceremonial ritual. In all important domestic ceremonies the priest must occupy the central position in the rituals that are performed. He embodies, as was stated earlier, the sacred knowledge and the sacred state of purity without which the ceremony itself has no magicoreligious efficacy. The Brahman priest is, in this sense, the *conferer*, the transmitter, of purity from its ultimate, highest source to its immediate, mundane context. This transmission of purity takes place (ideally) according to an order of preference: the secular Brahman has first priority, the Kshatriya second, the Vaisya next and the Sudra last, of course, in the sense that he cannot receive direct ministrations from the Brahman priest at all. We may say, then, that the Brahman dispenses ritual purity downward through the caste hierarchy while grain is dispensed upward as payment for this service.

However, both the Brahman priest and the domestic setting in which he performs his sacred duties must be in a specified state of purity before a ceremony can occur. From this standpoint it can be said that there must be an absence of the pollution that would otherwise defile the rituals, their setting, and their beneficiaries. This is achieved by engaging specialists who perform tasks (barbering, washing clothes, providing ceremonial objects, sweeping away dirt, etc.) which, in effect, 'drain away' pollution by causing it to be magically or symbolically absorbed by these specialists. Therefore, we may say that in opposition to the Brahman Priest (the dispenser of ritual purity *downward* in exchange for grain dispensed *upward*) there are simultaneously specialists who perform *contrapriestly functions*. That is, there are those who dispense ritual purity *upward* in exchange for grain dispensed *downward*. Priest and 'contrapriest' are absolutely opposed; they lie at the opposite extremes of the social hierarchy; they are mutually exclusive and this is symbolized by the fact that the ritual benefits they disburse and the remunerations they receive move always in opposite directions.

These oppositions are clearer when the terms *jajman* and *purjan* (=*kamin*=*kam karnewala*) are introduced. It will be remembered that in the *jajmani* system the *jajman* is the 'patron' who engages the services of a specialist, the latter being called a *purjan*. In the performance of his priestly duties, the Brahman is always a *purjan* vis a vis the Kshatriya and the Vaisya but never to a Sudra. As priest, the Brahman is never *jajman* to anyone. But the Brahman, and also the Kshatriya and Vaisya, in the context of pollution-removal, are *jajman* to the Sudra who, by virtue of his role of 'contrapriest', is *purjan* to all above him. At the poles of the hierarchy, then, both the Brahman and the Sudra are *purjan* in relation to all others with regard to their priestly functions and are *jajman* to no one. But this is not because they are the 'same'; it is because they are *opposite*.

Ritual services always flow away from the *purjan* and toward the *jajman*, whereas grain always flows away from the *jajman* and toward the *purjan*. Opposition is expressed in the fact that being a *purjan* in the interaction through which ritual purity is dispensed downward means being a *jajman* in the interaction through which ritual purity is dispensed upward. The giver of grain in one subsystem of the *jajmani* system is the giver of ritual service in the other, and vice versa.

The Kshatriya and Vaisya *varnas* occupy intermediary positions where they are neither exclusive dispensers of ritual purity nor of grain in a single direction in either sub-system of the ritual continuum. As ruler, the Kshatriya is the source of a certain measure of sacred as well as merely secular well-being. Historically, at least, there are some grounds for the king being seen as in an ambiguous position in this respect, the very sort of position one might expect to find under the circumstances—*viz.*, that the king is lower than the high yet higher than the low. In discussing 'legendary conflicts', Dumont (1962 : 56) observes:

> ... when the Kshatriya *Visvamitra* tries to appropriate the magical cow of the Brahman *Vasistha*, he is driven to

acknowledge that brute force is powerless against the magico-religious force which defends the right of the Brahman, and he finally decides to transform himself into a Brahman through austerities.

In other words, he opts out of his ambiguous status and becomes an unadulterated *purjan*. And even more clearly:

> I think we may conclude that while the *Ksatra*, or the king, has been dispossessed of religious functions, there are at the same time, at the core of the idea of kingship, elementary notions of a magico-religious nature which have not been 'usurped' by the Brahman. Below the orthodox brammanical level, another emerges on which, certainly in contact with popular mentality, the king has kept the magico-religious character which is universally inherent in his person and function. (p. 61).

To the extent that the Kshatriya can be said to possess a magico-religious character, to that extent his status as ruler can be interpreted in a manner that accords with our analytical scheme. That is, the Kshatriya is *jajman* to the Brahman in the latter's capacity as *purohit*, while simultaneously he is *purjan* to his subjects in the sense that his 'service' to them has a religious dimension. And conversely, of course, the ruler is also *purjan* (contrapriest) to the Brahman priest in his role of contractor of the impurities inherent in the occupation of kingship, while being *jajman* to those beneath him who bear the (contrapriestly) burdens of even deeper immersion in the pollution that pervades the physical world.

Finally, The Vaisyas are *jajman* to the Brahman and the Kshatriya in downward-devolving ritual purification, and *purjan* to no one, since Vaisyas are associated with no explicit priestly or political functions and since the Sudra is excluded from access to priestly services of any kind emanating from above. He is *jajman* to the Sudra in the context of upward evolving contrapriestly ritual services, of course, because his own access to the ultimate purification conferred by the Brahman would otherwise be blocked. The main elements of the logical structure underlying the *jajmani* system are summarized in Diagram I.

DIAGRAM I

Basic Oppositions Expressed in the Rendering of Ritual Services in the Hindu Jajmani System

		ECONOMIC CONTINUUM
Natural Purity (Varna Hierarchy)	Priest (Pure) PURJAN	JAJMAN
	Render ceremonial Services for Grain	Render Ceremonial Services for Grain
PURE — BRAHMAN / KSHATRIYA / VAISYA	Twice Born	PURJAN
	Give Grain for Ceremonies	
IMPURE — SUDRA	Once Born (excluded) JAJMAN	Contrapriest (Impure)
	RITUAL CONTINUUM	

In the economic continuum, the process of interaction utilizes the same 'grammatical principles' as does the ritual continuum. At first sight this might seem puzzling inasmuch as here we are dealing solely with getting fields plowed, tools made, clothing washed, hair cut, faces shaved, gold and silver jewelry cast, clay pots manufactured, dead animals removed, etc. The reason becomes clear, however, once it is recalled that ritual interaction occurs between the members of groups that are distinguished from one another *as groups* (i.e., possessors of common 'body particles') according to occupational criteria, and that it is the natural state of purity arising from attachment to a given occupation that determines *varna* status. Obviously, the natural state of purity which the *jatis* of any Twice Born *varna* require if they are to participate, as *jajmans* to Brahman *puroh'tas*, in orthodox rituals is heavily dependent on their capacity to avoid, through transfer downward, pollution inherent in types of work that are functionally essential to the operation of any peasant agricultural community. The ritual and economic continua are, in other words, interdependent, linked together by the concept of natural purity, and are therefore 'conjugated' in the same way.

The main difference between the two mutually supportive types of interaction is that in the economic domain priestly services and their ritual contexts are not directly at issue. What is at issue is the preservation of the natural purity which facilitates *access* to such services. In essence, therefore, the domain of economic interaction opposes the Twice Born to the Once Born; the former are ideally all *jajman* and the latter ideally all *purjan*; the one the avoiders of occupations entailing pollution of sufficient magnitude to bar interaction with the Brahman priest, the other the absorbers of pollution of this magnitude and therefore disbarred from such interaction except, as we have seen, in the capacity of 'contrapriests'. Grain and other material perquisites are transmitted downward as compensation for the upward transmission of purity through specialization in the performance of defiled occupations.

The fact that *jajman* status ideally coterminates with Twice Born *varna* status in the economic domain has, I think, been responsible for one of the most persistent oversimplifications which students of Indian society have perpetuated over the years.

I refer to the tendency to equate *jajman* status with 'dominant caste' and thereby to create the impression that *jajmans* are invariably members of an exploiter class. The oversimplification becomes immediately apparent where empirical investigations reveal that not only a 'dominant caste's' members are *jajmans* but that the members of *most* castes are *jajmans* under various conditions. (See Chapter 6) It becomes even more apparent when we take account of *purjan* status. For if *jajmans* are an exploiter class, then Brahman priests and Untouchables both belong to an *exploited* (*purjan*) class! And what is equally as perplexing, intermediate castes simultaneously qualify as both 'exploiters' (*jajman*) and 'exploited' (*purjan*).

Obviously, the way out of such absurdities is the realization that *the ritual and economic domains are separate subsystems* each manifesting distinctive oppositions between *jajman* and *purjan*, each representing specific applications of the 'grammar' of Hindu sacred law. Dominance, as Srinivas (1952) has defined it, is a concept that is rooted in materialistic considerations; it is the net product of varying combinations and degrees of political, demographic and economic superiority, coupled with the determination to symbolically ratify this dominance in Hindu terms. That is, it is expressive of a formidable but not an exclusive capacity to enjoy *jajman* status in the economic domain as a necessary precondition of enjoying some combination of *jajman* and *purjan* status in the ritual domain. An exploitative component of *jajmani* status clearly exists in the economic domain for here *purjans* consist of *jatis* which have historically become identified with defiling tasks (i.e., the absorption of impurity, a negatively evaluated state) because they have always lacked the power to avoid falling prey to this fate. In the ritual domain, however, as we have seen, *purjans* are not confined to *jatis* of exploited Sudras. The category also includes the Brahmans and the Kshatriya. The crucial element here is a pattern of reciprocal interaction among groups whose hierarchical relationships and specialized functions have been fixed and stabilized by the facts (consequences) of economic inequality and diversification. Its purpose is religious: To achieve salvation in accordance with the methods for doing so which proceed from the assumptions about the cosmos which underlie Hindu Civilization. This is effectuated by the performance of ceremonies in which involvement with biological process (the source of defilement) is overcome through the ritual ministrations of two types of *purjan*—*viz.*, priestly dispensers of purity and contrapriestly absorbers of impurity—for the benefit of a salvation-seeking clientele (*jajmans*).

IV

The tribes of the Nilgiri Hills have long been known to have produced in a semi-aboriginal setting many of the essential relationships associated with caste and *jajmani* interaction in Civilized India. It is obvious, even on superficial examination, that this is not fortuitous, these tribes are, after all, part of the Sub-continent's population and have always enjoyed social contact with the encompassing Indian Civilization. There has nevertheless been considerable debate over just how faithfully the Nilgiri case reproduced the structure of traditional Hindu social interaction. This debate may be settled, it seems to me, if it is shown that Nilgiri economic interaction does not merely bear a superficial resemblance to the Hindu *jaj nani* system, but that it actually rather faithfully replicates the 'grammatical rules' of Hindu sacred law just as does its plains counterpart. Differences existing between the two, I propose to demonstate, are in details which inevitably arise from the fact that Nilgiri society is a social world of its own, set in a remote corner of the Indian environment, and characterized by an essentially tribal level of technology and form of social organization.

In this discussion, I shall make abundant references to an article by Richard C. Fox (1963) written for the purpose of criticising a contention made by Lewis (1955), Beidelman (1959) and this author (Gould 1957) at one point in his thinking that the 'dominant caste' in a *jajmani* system must invariably be a landowning caste. For although I do not agree entirely with his arguments, and hope to show where I feel his reasoning has gone awry, Fox has compiled a useful survey of the literature on Nilgiri economic interaction.

Speaking in the ethnographic present, there are five tribes in the Nilgiri Hills of South India that are bound together in a state of economic symbiosis: the Toda, the Badaga, the Kota, the Kurumba and the Irula. Each tribe displays many of the attributes associated with castes on the plains. They are endogamous; they observe numerous commensal restrictions vis-a-vis one another; they are occupationally specialized; and most of all, they are arranged in a hierarchy which implies different degrees of pollution.

At the top of this hierarchy are the Toda. They are a pastoral tribe who maintain herds of buffaloes and specialize in operating dairies whose chief end-product is *ghi* (clarified butter), an important ceremonial item in Hindu India. Next come the Badaga which practices agriculture and seems to have always been the chief food producer in the hills. After them are the Kota whose contribution to the Nilgiri division of labor is the performance of artisan services, although some Kota also practice agriculture as well. The lowest rung in the hierarchy is occupied by two hunting and gathering tribes, the Kurumba and the Irula, who dispense forest products. Of the two, the Kurumbas are by far the more important. "The Irulas," says Fox (1963:497), "seem to play only a minor role, and observers have tended to lump them together with the Kurumbas "

The ordering of the tribes in this manner accords very well with the basic assumptions about the world and the cosmos which we earlier ascribed to Hindu Civilization on the plains, and with the concept of natural purity which flows from these assumptions. Thus, Toda paramountcy is based upon the fact that they are custodians of a sacred animal, the buffalo, which is ritually sacrificed on certain ceremonial occasions, is given as a sacred gift on others, and is the source of the sacred substance, *ghi*. It is also based upon the supernatural aura which surrounds the Toda dairies and the power and prestige enjoyed throughout the hills by the Toda dairy priests (*palol*). In other words, the Toda are structurally analogous to the Brahman caste on the plains, and the dairy priest to the Brahman priest; and like the latter, their status is derived from the successful avoidance of the polluting implications of involvement in 'mundane' occupations, and the transmission of purity downward through the social system by the performance of rituals.

Despite Fox's assertions to the contrary, the Badaga are structurally analogous to the landowning agricultural castes of the plains as far as their position in the *jajmani* system is concerned. That is, they are farmers who produce the grain that is one of the chief ingredients in the operation of the complex pattern of economic and ritual exchanges which comprise its essence. And they are typical of the 'clean castes' in general, all of whom enjoy *jajmani* status in the economic subsystem of the *jajmani* system as a necessary precondition of maintaining the degree of natural purity which facilitates enjoying some combination of *jajman* and *purjan* status in the ritual subsystem. That the Badaga are not in possession of land tenures identical to those found among the Hindu *kisan* castes, and lack the kind of dominance characteristic of the Kshatriya and their political equivalents in the areas of high civilization may be true. But these differences do not involve what is central to the determination of status in a *jajmani* system. The central consideration is *position relative to the priest* (the dispenser of purity)* and thus the quality of the relationship which may be enjoyed with him in the context of ritual. Dominant castes on the plains are never ranked higher, but indeed are always ranked lower, than the Brahmans (except when the dominant caste is Brahman, but even then secular Brahmans are less pure than priests); they are *jajmans* to Brahmans only in the ritual continuum, and in this context *jajman* status *vis-a-vis* the priest implies subordinate not superordinate status. This is the case with the Badaga as well. We may say that in both the economic and ritual domains, structurally speaking, the Badaga are to the Toda in the Nilgiris what the ordinary Twice Born are to the Brahmans on the plains.

The 'artisan tribe', the Kota, occupies the third position in the scale. Their marked differentiation from the agriculturalist Badaga and assignment to a lower ranked stratum appears to me to represent an interesting variation on the 'grammar' of Hindu sacred law. For on the plains, the artisan castes, especially the metal smiths (*Lohar*) and carpenters (*Barhai*), do in fact rank somewhat below the traditional agriculturalist castes like *Ahir* and *Kurmi*, but they are not regarded as being sufficiently ritually distinct to warrant assignment to a separate *varna*. Yet the reasons for their greater

*A point made by Bougle long ago and reintroduced in modern sociology by Dumont and Pocock (1958).

differentiation in the Nilgiris nevertheless seems entirely compatible with the assumptions about the ritual implications of involvement with biological process ('blood, death and dirt') which underlie Hinduism. For it is said that the Kota eat carrion, a practice which the Badaga do not pursue and which would presumably mean that the Kota possess markedly less natural purity than the former (Fox 1963: 497).

'Not all Kotas,' relates Fox (*Ibid*:497), "are engaged in handicrafts; some are given over completely to agriculture." Apparently the real significance of this fact, although it is not brought out by Fox or any of the sources he cites, is that Kotas who adopt agriculture are engaged in a Nilgiri version of 'sanskritization' (Srinivas 1952). Fox merely states (*Ibid*.: 497) that these Kotas give "grain to the Toda, presumably in return for *ghi*," instead of providing artisan services as would otherwise be normal. I suspect, however, that even more importantly, the Kota who became agriculturalists couple this with absetention from further consumption of carrion and a claim of status-parity with the Badaga. This, at least, is an hypothesis worth investigating because it follows logically from the 'model' of *jajmani* interaction which the Nilgiri tribes somehow managed to acquire from encompassing Hindu Civilization and apply to their own social relations.

The full religious implications of the Kurumba and Irula for the inter-tribal caste system of the Nilgiri Hills have apparently not been properly examined by anyone. It is clear from Fox's survey that the two hunting and gathering tribes embody in the minds of the other participants in the system deeply repellant qualities, although it would not be appropriate to conclude that the Kurumba and Irula are actually designated as Untouchables. The basis of their repugnance to the others seems vaguely connected with a notion that forest dwellers have low natural purity because of ther familiarity with sorcery and witchcraft. The Kurumba and Irula participate in both the economic and ritual subsystems of the Nilgiri *jajmani* system, and one gathers rather more in the latter than in the former, though information is so sketchy that one cannot be really sure. Fox's (1963:497) conclusion is that the "Kurumbas (Irulas) interact in this system to a lesser extent than the other three," and that the forest tribes' "relations with the

Badagas are more intimate than those with other groups, although Shortt (1869:256) maintains that they perform services for the Todas."

These latter observations are useful because they suggest a Sudra-like status for the Kurumbas and Irulas in that the ritually highest tribe in the system, the Toda, are said to have more limited interactions with them than the ritually lower Badaga. Moreover, when we examine the ritual continuum of the Nilgiri *jajmani* system it will be seen that the nature of the Kurumba and Irula participation in Nilgiri rituals strongly suggests that they perform a *contrapriestly* role in some ways analogous to that of certain Sudra castes on the plains. We do not, after all, expect to find complete identity of social structure between the two jajmani systems, but only a *consistency* of structure which arises from the application of common principles of religio-economic interaction derived from a common referent—*viz.*, assumptions about the nature of the cosmos and the world in which Hinduism is rooted.

In this very connection, it is necessary to point out that the exchange of commodities in the economic subsystem of the Nilgiri *jajmani* system, although infused with the same mingling of sacred and secular implications (*viz.*, the stabilization of differential degrees of natural purity, and the simple exchange of usable economic goods) does not occur on exactly the same terms as on the plains. We have seen in the latter instance how Brahmans acting as *jajmans* pay grain (and things that stand for it) just as other Twice Born castes do for the rendering of contrapriestly (*purjan*) services by lower status castes. This enables them to transmit purity down the hierarchical scale to the 'border' of the Once Born *Varna* by officiating as priests (*purjans*) at the ceremonies of the Twice Born who correspondingly assume the role of *jajmans* and reimburse them in grain. Thus, we were able to conceptualize the Hindu *jajmani* system as in a sense a set of oppositions between grain-dispensing *jajmans* and grain-receiving *purjans*.

Among the Nilgiri tribes, however, only the Badaga and 'sanskritized' (i.e., agriculturalist) Kota pay grain for commodities and ritual services. The Toda obviously do not because they do not practice agriculture, even indirectly as landlords. Instead, the Toda preserve an entirely non-agricultural technology, pastoralism, and exalt this technology into the very exemplification of their religious superiority. They symbolize this religious superiority and ritual dominance over the other tribes by their production of *ghi*, a 'pure' and comparatively not very utilitarian substance, which they then use as their 'currency' for obtaining grain from the Badaga and agriculturalized Kota, artisan services from the regular Kota, and forest products from the Kurumba and Irula. In a sense that is not true of the grain dispensed to *purjans* by plains Brahmans, *ghi* dispensed by the Toda appears to have *in itself* some measure of sacred potency. In the exchange of economic goods *per se* the Toda contribution is set apart by its non-utilitarian opposition to the more straight-forwardly utilitarian contributions of the other tribes, and by the apartness of the technology which creates it. And, most intriguingly, the same holds true for the obversely situated Kurumba and Irula. Their economic and contrapriestly functions are also generated by a technology which is in marked contrast to the other tribes, and although the commodities they contribute to the Nilgiri economy cannot be said to be 'esoteric' in the sense that *ghi* is, they are nevertheless seen as the harvest of a region (the forest) which is thought to be laden with dark and dangerous powers.

The evidence suggests to me, however, that just as the agricultural castes have been a kind of focal point of economic distribution in the *jajmani* system in Hindu India, in the sense that it has been they who have always 'purchased' with grain (*anaj*) the 'commodity' (freedom from pollution) which priest and contrapriest had to 'sell', it is the Badaga (and their Kota emulators) who are its economic focal point in the Nilgiris. Badagas are farmers whose households contract service ties with households of specialists among other tribes. Like the plains *jajmani* system, "the interrelationships of the 'tribes' are on a familial or village, rather than a tribal, level" (Fox 1963: 497) and payment for services (also like on the plains) is in the form of a systematic share of each harvest, called the *gudu* (a Kanarese world meaning 'basket' or 'nest'—see Fox *Ibid.*, 501). The Badaga pay for *ghi* and priestly services from the Toda in this way, and pay in the same manner their (contrapriestly) Kota and Kurumba/Irula *purjans*. Further illustrating the extent to which the Nilgiri *jajmani* system is an 'organizational analogue' of its Hindu counterpart is Fox's (*Ibid.*; 498) observation that :

> Each Badaga village has a *muttu kotas* in surrounding Kota villages who does artisan work for various Badaga families, and who receives the grain payment at harvest time. . . . These *muttu Kotas* also serve the Todas, Kurumbas and Irulas.

Fox will disagree with my views about the Badaga, of course, because he contends that in the Nilgiris it is the non-agricultural Toda who are the focal point of the system. This is because he cannot see evidence that the Badaga possess any of the 'coercive powers' allegedly associated with dominant agricultural castes on the plains. His error lies in a failure to realize that in the *jajmani* syst m of both cultures there is a *reciprocal* pattern of dominance and dependence. Todas and Badagas, like Brahmans and the 'clean' agricultural castes, are both clients (*purjans*) and patrons (*jajmans*) under different circumstances; dominance in one continunm of symbolically opposed interaction (as when a Toda requires grain from his Badaga *jajman*) contrasts with subordination in another (as when a Badaga serves as a procurer of objects for a Toda sacred dairy — *cf.*, Fox 1963:500). Coercion itself becomes a relative matter because materialistically-based dominance may be characteristic in one subsystem while supernaturally-based dominance is characteristic in another. The fact that observers and students of Nilgiri economic interaction never picked up these nuances of structure in the *jajmani* system probably accounts in great measure for their fairly uniform conclusion that the Toda are the unambiguously dominant 'caste' in the hills. Fox refers the reader to accounts by Finicio (1603),* Hough (1829), Harkness (1832), Shortt (1869), King (1870) and Mandelbaum (1941) in support of the Toda-dominance thesis. All of the cited authors say in one way or another what Hough (1829:60) is quoted as saying: "The other classes regard them [the Toda] as the lords of these regions, and the Buddagurs have paid

---

*Quoted in Rivers (1906).

tribute to them from the period of their first settlement in the neighborhood." (Fox 1963:502)

Yet, interestingly, Fox himself found instances of contrary perceptions of Toda relationships with the other tribes which he explains away as relating to the period following the arrival of the British when the *jajmani* system in its "pristine" form began to break down. Rivers (1906:362), for example, is quoted to the effect that the Badaga "looked on the tribute of grain to the Toda as given of their own good will, while a similar tribute to the Kurumbas was dictated by the fear of the consequences of sorcery." In like manner, Emeneau (1938:105) found that although the Kotas have "a relatively low position yet [they] do not feel themselves much inferior to the Badagas and certainly will not openly admit any inferiority." Harkness who in one context (1832:85) has had attributed to him by Fox (1963:504) the statement that the Toda assumes a posture of 'superiority which the Burgher [Badaga] has no inclination to dispute," is also quoted as saying that the Badaga "did not recognize any Toda right to levy *gudu* on them at any specific rate or ratio, although they did recognize the institution of *gudu*, and were willing to give it still," but "according to their own wants and fancies." (Fox's paraphrasing of Harkness and Breeks—1873:12).

We cannot dismiss the possibility, in the light of the conclusions we have drawn about the assumptions and logic underlying *jajmani* interaction, that the inconsistencies which appear in these early accounts arose not from the consequences of British rule but from the authors' lack of adequate understanding of the system they were describing. For it appears very likely that whereas the Toda would, in terms of their degree of natural purity and their role as priests, be, in Hough's apt words, the 'lords' of the region, it would also be likely that the Badaga and the Kota have felt a certain reciprocal power over the Toda in their capacity as *jajmans* (i.e., dispensers of grain and artisan services respectively) to them.

The Badaga fear of the Kurumba which, we noted above, had been observed by Emeneau points toward the same conclusion. Surely the Badaga feel no deference toward the Kurumba on materialistic grounds, yet they fear them. The reason, declared Emeneau, is sorcery. In other words, for *supernatural* reasons (that is, in their contrapriestly capacity) the Kurumba enjoy a kind of dominance over the Badaga despite the latter's superiority over them in economic terms and in degree of natural purity. Application of this reasoning, i.e., application of the 'grammar' of Hindu sacred law, to all the observed relationships among the Niligiri tribes would probably clarify most of the seeming inconsistencies in the accounts which have been given of them.

The extent to which the Niligiri *jajmani* system is a replication in principle of its plains counterpart is most thoroughly appreciated when one examines the operation of its ritual subsystem. As Fox puts it (1963:498), in the Nigiris "there is a strong factor of ceremonial and supernatural interdependence... Each group is integrated into the heart of the ritual and ceremony of the others."

As on the plains, funerals are understandably crucial occasions for activating ritual relationships between the tribes whose purpose is the correct handling of the pollution problems attendant on death. In these relationships the basic opposition between pure and impure which underlies the *jajmani* system appears time and time again. Actually, these oppositions have a locus within the Toda tribe itself, in their moiety organization which divides the tribe into two endogamous divisions called *Tartharol* and *Teivaliol*. Between these two divisions there is expressed in miniature the same principles of opposition and their underlying cultural meanings as are found in the wider *jajmani* system. "Thus, at a Toda funeral," says Fox (1963:499), "various rituals are carried out by the *Teivaliol* if the deceased is a *Tartharol*, and vice versa."

Whereas it is through the moiety organization of the tribe that priestly services are obtained from a group not implicated in the pollution of death, and therefore *opposed* to it, it is through the Kota, Kurumba and Irula that contrapriestly, defilement-removing services are obtained. Kota musicians must play at a Toda green funeral (Fox 1963:498) and, much more significantly, must provide a *burial shroud* for the deceased (*Ibid.*:498). At a Toda dry funeral, the Kota must supply "a cloak, 8 annas for embroidering it (done by the Toda women), a bow and 3 arrows, a knife, a sieve, and a buffalo." (*Ibid.*:498) Kurumbas also entertain at Toda funderals and "provide the

Todas with 2 ceremonial objects: a tall pole used at funeral services and afterwards burnt, and the post upon which the buff aloes are sacrificed." (*Ibid.*:499) And, quite strikingly, not to mention *understandably* from the standpoint of the principles of Hindu sacred law, Rivers is reported as stating that "the Kurumbas play no other role in the social life of the Todas." (*Ibid.* : 499)

It is significant that the Badaga are not indicated as playing any contra priestly roles in Toda funerals, for this makes sense if they are structurally analogous to the Twice Born on the Plains. This view is reinforced by such observations as that, "the Kotas perform much the same role at Badaga funerals as at those of the Todas." (*Ibid.* : 499) It is also reinforced by the obverse observation that Toda and Badaga both play purity-conferring roles at Kota funerals. "At a Kota green funeral," declares Fox (*Ibid*:498), "Todas and Badagas attend and bring 2 or or 3 male buffalo calves or some cloth as offerings," while at dry funerals, "buffaloes or cows are brought." At other ceremonies too both Toda and Badaga attend, the former offering *ghi* and the latter grain.

The *palol*, or Toda dairy priest, by all accounts, enjoys *purjan* status in the ritual continuum of the Nilgiri *jajmani* system vis-a-vis all the other tribes, as our structural analysis would lead us to expect. Fox quotes Marshall (1873:145) to the effect that dairy priests could be observed moving in the Badaga villages "obliging the people, through influence of his supposed powers of witchcraft, and the great sanctity attaching to his person, to comply with his demands for little luxuries of food, and for the grain due to his [dairy] as Kutu." Rivers (1906:102) said that, "All the grain the *palol* or priest eats must be given by the Badagas." And, says Fox (Ibid.: 500);

> Harkness was told that this grain portion ... is in return for the prayers of the *palol*. The Badagas say their crops and cattle would not do well without the priest's blessing.

Nor would the Badagas' crops do well without the contra-priest's blessing, it seems. For Breeks (1873:53) is cited (Fox 1963:499) to the effect that each "Badaga *gramma*" has a Kurumba priest "who performs annual ceremonies for the

Badagas at sowing and harvest time, and is called in on all occasions of blight and murrain to propitiate or scare the demon of desease." Furthermore, Harkness (1832:56-7) mentions agricultural rites which certain Kurumbas perform for the Badagas where "they ritually initiate plowing by sacrificing a goat (provided by the Badagas), and then ceremonially plow 10 to 12 paces." (Fox 1963:499) "They also initiate sowing and reaping," states Fox (*Ibid.*:499), and they "prescribe medicines, and remove hexes from crops and people." These activities so closely parallel the contrapriestly functions of various Sudra *jatis* on the plains that further comment is quite unnecessary.

Therefore, it appears safe to conclude that the Nilgiri tribes indeed have a *jajmani* systen in the full sense of the word. By this I mean that it is underlyingly an expression of assumptions concerning the nature of the world and the cosmos that are products of the Hindu world view. Since the Niligiri social world cannot be said to be explicitly Hindu, we must assume that it was the 'logic' and the underlying assumptions of Hindu sacred law which somehow diffused into this world, divorced in the main from the detailed cultural content of plains Hindu Civilization. The consequent structural comparability of the Hindu and Nilgiri *jajmani* systems is to be found, to refer once again to the proponents of a 'Sociology of India', at the level of relations between features and the principles governing these relations.

Fox seems to me to have gone wrong in his discussion of the Nilgiri material for at least two reasons. First, he appears to be unduly enamored of 'materialistic' explanations of power relations by which, in the last analysis, he seems actually to mean economic explanations in the Marxist style. Fox says as much at one point. Rejecting other peoples' attempts to explain the sources of Toda power over the other tribes in supernaturalistic terms as a "cultural or psychological argument'" he contends that this "cannot serve as an explanation of social structure." Yet, not even in the high Hindu Civilization on the plains can the power of the Brahman, which is the real structural equivalent of the Toda's power in the Nilgiris, be accounted for in purely materialistic, or economic deterministic, terms.

The second point, then, is this very lack of appreciation of the religious roots and implications of both *jajmani* systems. As I have said, the Toda and the *palol*, or Toda dairy priest, embody the same religious values and meanings in the Nilgiri Hills as the Brahman caste and the Brahman priest do on the plains. The Toda is the recipient of *jajmani* for the same reason that the Brahman is. Both dispense ritual purity (a powerful *supernatural* agent) downward through the social hierarchy in their capacity as priest (*purjan*). In terms of their internal efforts to preserve their superior state of natural purity, of course, both are *jajmans* as well, but this in relation to a different subsystem of the *jajmani* system. What has to be appreciated, it seems to me, is the power of belief systems. In the Nilgiris, as on the plains, the whole religious system is internalized by all who take part in *jajmani* interaction. This means that the supernatural power attributed to buffaloes, dairies and *palols* is implicitly believed in by all parties to the system, by the Todas who profit most from these beliefs as much as by the Badagas, Kotas, Kurumbas and Irulas who profit less from them, or at least differently. The fear of the Toda dairy by the other tribes is the fear of *believers* in the supernatural sanctity and potency of the priest. But is the fear which the Toda, Badaga and Kota have of the contra-priestly powers of their Kurumba *purjans* any the less real? The point is that the Nilgiri *jajmani* system is precisely what the word implies—a *system*, composed of reciprocal relationships and shared beliefs whose fundamental assumptions and organizational principles have somehow been inherited from Hindu society on the plains.

BIBLIOGRAPHY

Beidelman, Thomas O., *A Comprative Analysis of the Jajmani System*, New York : Association of Asian Studies, Monograph No. VIII, 1959.

Bougle, C., 'The Essence and Reality of the Caste System,' in Louis Dumont and David Pocock, eds., *Contributions to Indian Sociology*, No. II, The Hague: Mouton & Co., 1958.

Breeks, James Wilkenson, *An Account of the Primitive Tribes and Monuments of the Nilagiris*, edited by his wife, London: W. Hallen, 1873.

Dumont, Louis, 'The Conception of Kingship,' in Louis Dumont and David Pocock, eds., *Contributions to Indian Sociology*, No. VI, The Hague: Mouton & Co., 1962.

Dumont, Louis and David Pocock, 'For a Sociology of India,' in Louis Dumont and David Pocock, eds., *Contributions to Indian Sociology*, No. I, The Hugue, Mouton & Co., 1957.

Dumont, Louis and David Pocock, eds., *Contributions to Indian Sociology*, No. II, The Hague: Mouton & Co., 1958.

Durkheim, Emile, *The Elementary Forms of Religious Life*, Glencoe, III., The Free Press, 1947.

———, and Marcel Mause, *Primit've Classification* (Translated by Rodney Needham), London, 1963.

Emeneau, M.B., 'Toda Culture 35 Years After: An Acculturation Study,' *Annals. Bhandarkar Oriental Research Institute*, vol. XIX, 1938.

Fox, Richard G., 'Caste Dominance and Coercion in the Nilgiries, *Papers of the Michigan Academy of Science, Arts, and Letters*, vol. XLVIII: 493-512, 1963.

Gould, Harold A., 'The Hindu Jajmani System: a Case of Economic Particularism, *Southwestern Journal of Anthropology*, vol. 14, 428-437, 1958. (Chapter 5 in this Volume).

———, 'A Jajmani System of North India: its Structure, Magnitude and Meaning,' *Ethnology*, vol. III: 12-41, 1964. (Chapter 6 in this Volume).

———, 'Castes, Outcastes and the Sociology of Stratification,' in K. Ishwaran, ed., *The Sociology of Caste*, Oxford: Pergamon Press, 1967. (This is a revision of the original article with this title which appeared in the *International Journal of Comparative Sociology*, vol. 1: 220-238, 1960). (Chapter 3 in this Volume).

Harkness, Henry, *A Description of a Singular Aboriginal Race Inhabiting the Summit of the Neilgherry Hills or Blue Mountains of Coimbatore in the Southern Peninsula of India*, London: Smith, Elder, 1832.

Hough, James, *Letters on the Climate, Inhabitants, Productions. Etc. Etc. of the Neilgherries or Blue Mountains of Coimbatore. South India*, London: J. Eatchard & Son, 1829.

Hume, Robert E., *The Thirteen Principal Upanishads*, Bombay: Oxford University Press, 1934.

King, W. Ross, *The Aboriginal Tribes of the Nilgiri Hills*, London: Longman, Green & Co., 1870.

Levi-Strauss, Claude, *Totemism*, Boston: Beacon Press, 1962.

———, 'The Bear and the Barber,' *Journal of the Royal Anthropological Institute*, vol. 93, 1-11, 1963.

Lewis, Oscar and Victor Bernuew, 'Caste and the Jajmani System in a North Indian Village,' *Scientific Monthly*, vol. 83, 1955.

Mandelbaum, David C., 'Culture Change Amcng the Nilgiri Tribes,' *American Anthropologist*, vol. 43, 1941.

Marshall, William E., *A Phrenologist Amongst the Todas or the Study of a Primitive Tribe in South India*, London, Longman, Green & Co., 1873.

Orenstein, Henry, 'The Structure of Hindu Caste Values: A Preliminary Study of Hierarchy and Ritual Defilement,' *Ethnology*, vol. 4: 1-15, 1965a.

———, 'Toward a Grammar of Defilement in Hindu Sacred Law,' presented at a *Conference on Social Structure and Social Change in India: Methods and Results*, June 3-5, 1965.

Passin, Herbert 'Untouchability in the Far East, *Monumenta Nipponica*, vol. XI, 27-47, 1955.

Pocock, David, 'Difference' in East Africa: a Study of Caste and Religion in Modern Indian Society,' *Southwestern Journal of Anthropology*, vol. 13, 1957.

Rivers, W.H.R., *The Todas*, London; Macmillan Co., 1906.

Schweitzer, Albert, *Indian Thought and its Development*, Boston: Beacon Press, 1957.

Shortt, J., 'An Account of the Hill Tribes of the Neilgherries;' *Transactions of the Ethnological Society of London*, vol. VII, (1869)

Srinivas: M.N., 'A Note on Sanskritization and Westernization,' *Far Eastern Quarterly*, vol. 15: 481-496, 1952.

Swanson, Guy E., *The Birth of the Gods: The Origin of Primitive Beliefs*, Ann Arbor, Michigan: University of Michigan Press, 1960.

5

The Hindu Jajmani System: A Case of Economic Particularism

This chapter deals with the system of traditional economic relationships, called the Jajmani System, which is a widespread feature of the peasant village culture of India. The analysis is based partly on field work which I undertook in the north Indian village of Sherupur (a pseudonym) in 1954-55 and partly on secondary sources. Although by no means capable of illuminating all of the important aspects and implications of nonpecuniary patterns of economic interaction in rural Indian life, it is hoped that what follows will add to the reader's understanding of such patterns.

I

The precise character of economic relationships in the villages of India is determined by the complex division of labor that exists there and by the particular set of religious attitudes which underlie and perpetuate that division of labor. Up to a point, Indian villages are not unlike the peasant-agricultural communities one finds anywhere in the world. (cf. Redfield, 1930, 1941, 1950, 1955, 1956; Firth, 1946, 1952; Lewis, 1951; Embree, 1946, etc.). That is, they contain a group of families, usually compound in structure, residentially centralized in the midst of their agricultural lands. Technology is simple and productivity low; poverty is extensive and life centers around the quest for subsistence. The pursuit of material selfsufficiency is associated with a general centripetal orientation to life in both the family and the community. But in India, although all villages are primarily dependent upon subsistence agricultural production, all families do not practice agriculture directly. Only a certain proportion do so while the rest specialize in various craft and menial occupations. In exchange for these various services the cultivators pay a systematically determined share of their produce to those providing them.

At the heart of rural India's complex division of labor is caste. Compound patrifamilies are the loci of rural productivity and these are ritually subdivided into endogamous clusters in accordance with the moral valuation which the Hindu Religion places upon their occupational activities. The criterion of ritual evaluation is whether or not the caste occupation, or perhaps more accurately *the configuration of caste functions*, does or does not subject its practitioners to ritual contamination. Roughly, those clusters of patrifamilies whose work activities put them in continuous contact with "blood, death, and dirt" (Passin, 1955), singly or in combination, are regarded as "unclean" castes and must avoid connubial, commensal, and many other forms of social contacts with those clusters of patrifamilies who are "clean". The latter are called Twice Born castes because their males may experience the second, or spiritual, birth of initiation into the sacrosanct community of ritually pure Hindus. Basically, the distinction is between the land-owning, cultivating castes, on the one hand, who dominate the social order and the landless craft and menial castes, on the other, who are subordinate within it. Hinduism elaborately rationalizes and congeals this fundamental distinction.

What must not be overlooked as one views this caste system, however, which Kinglsey Davis (1951) regards as the most thoroughgoing attempt of all time to make "absolute inequality" the basis of social relationships, is that the unclean occupations are just as necessary to the Hindu's concept of community life as are the clean ones. In other words, castes who remove dead animals are Untouchable on that account but they are also intrinsically essential to the Hindu social system because the Twice Borns are ritually prevented from performing this unclean occupation. By the same token, *all* unclean occupations are at once degrading to their practitioners

THE HINDU JAJMANI SYSTEM 137

yet essential to the appropriate organization of any orthodox Hindu community. Ritual purity for some can be maintained only at the expense of defilement for others where, as in India, the criteria of ritual status are the fundamental occupational functions required to enable the community to operate.

Villages like Sherupur, therefore, must face and resolve a social structural dilemma towards which the Hindu social system predisposes Indian community life. Such centripetal principles as the corporate or joint family, caste endogamy, face-to-face interpersonal relations, distrust of the impersonal "outside", etc., make avoidance-orientations a pervasive aspect of the peasant's life. The wrong contact, the wrong deed, can lead to ritual contamination, outcasting, and expulsion from the ancestral community. On the other hand, these very social structural features which give such power to avoidance-orientations are the same ones which make inter-familial, intercaste, and inter-village contacts inescapable. For since the sources of contamination are also the sources for the Twice Born castes of essential goods and services which they may not provide for themselves, systematic ways of overriding the divisive potentialities of caste, while at the same time preserving the institution itself, must exist if the community is to survive in a manner which preserves its Hindu moral premises.

We may put the issue this way: Contacts with "outsiders" (non-kin, other castes, other villagers, etc) who may be ritually defiling are feared yet recognized as essential for a number of purposes; which in turn necessitates the establishment of formal social mechanisms capable of reconciling the urge to avoid social intercourse for religious reasons with the need to establish and maintain it for instrumental reasons. Social structure like the *Gaon Panchayat* (Council of Elders) achieve this reconciliation at the political level in rural India; the so-called jajmani system does so at the economic level.

Declares Wiser:

> A social organization such as the Hindu caste system, which gives each occupational group a fixed standing within the community, must of necessity have certain patterns of behavior which enable each caste to maintain its own status and satisfactorily engage in relationships with others. Among

these behavior patterns are marriage, social intercourse in matters of eating, drinking and smoking, conventions of untouchability and unapproachability, and service (jajmani) relationships.

II

The world of the Indian peasant is heavily laden with kinship values. Much of his life is spent within the ambit of the corporate family and its extensions which is in turn bound to its traditional (ancestral) village. Most of the people who supervise the peasant's activities and whose activities he in turn supervises are kin of varying degrees and are ordinarily members of the common household. Movement beyond the confines of the village is often predetermined by the location of affinal and consanguineal kin whom one has elsewhere. Within the village, inter-familial interaction takes place among families who have ordinarily been in continuous association for generations. In short, the kinship system contsitutes the framework within which the peasant carries on those relationships which from his standpoint possess the highest measure of trustworthiness, durability, and meaningfulness.

When, therefore, a person must venture outside the confines of his own kinship unit, he tends wherever possible to establish with whomever he encounters ties which approximate as nearly as possible those customary between genuine kin. This is an expression of the idea implicit in the peasant's mind that the most stable relationships in one's life are those based on kinship.

When villagers must deal with strangers, [says Marriott] (1955, p. 248), they have the choice of including the stranger either in a family or in an intercaste type of relationship. If strangers are thrown together anonymously as in a bus or in an urban shop and if their common activities are casual ones, then they may classify each other by relative age as pseudokinsmen. Ultimately they may trace more specific connections through villages with which they share real family relationships.

These are the premises which underlie the kind of ties which get established among participants in the jajmani system. Faced with the necessity of bringing families of different castes and, therefore, of different ritual status, into stable economic interaction, without at the same time contaminating each other, certain principles of kinship organization are brought into operation. The manner in which this is done represents the culture's answer to the need for extrafamilial and extravillage interaction for the attainment of economic ends consistent with the Hindu moral order.

Naturally, all possible components of kin relationships are not projected into the organization of the jajmani system. Only those which have relevance to its particular problems and aims have been selected. They pertain (a) to the patterning of superordinate-subordinate relations between *jajmans* (patrons) and their *purjans* or *kam karewalas* (workers, suppliers of services. etc.), (b) to the range of commitments between participants, and (c) to the temporal continuity of the relationships established.

Families of the clean castes (Twice Born) are the patrons, the *jajmans*, while the unclean castes (Sudra and Untouchable) are the *purjans*, the providers of services. In short, it is a matter of land-owning, wealth-and power-controlling high castes providing a structurally fixed share of their agricultural produce, along with numerous "considerations," in exchange for craft and menial services rendered by the mainly landless, impoverished, politically weak lower castes. The latter thereby absorb the onus of ritual contamination associated with the tasks they perform and facilitate the ritual purity and consequent moral apotheosis of the former. They are at once outside the ritual pale yet essential to the functional pale of Hindu society.

This superordinate-subordinate dimension of the jajmani system is primarily paternalistic and secondarily pecuniary in its basis. It is a matter of a particular *jajman* engaging the services of a particular *purjan* who thereby obligates himself to maintain this tie in perpetuity as long as both discharge their diffuse set of responsibilities to each other. Sons of each family are expected to continue the relationship into the succeeding generation, as are son's sons etc, while preserving intact all of its power, ritual, and material implications. A *purjan* must defer to, respect, and defend his *jajman* (ideally, of course), as well as serve him, in a way strongly analogous to the manner in which a son of a corporate family is expected to orient himself to the father. Put briefly, a *purjan* is to his *jajman* as a son is to his father, at least in the formal respects which have been enumerated above.

The term "considerations" is Wiser's and refers to those features of the jajmani system which in his view lie at its heart and explain the peasant's preference for it over more rationalized economic relations. This may be, and we will examine the nature of these "considerations" in a moment, but no doubt of equal importance is the fact that these "considerations" symbolize the fact that the jajmani tie is personal, face-to-face; that it involves not merely a carefully accounted exchange between a buyer and a seller, but also a plethora of explicit and implicit commitments *between two families* very like, in comprehensiveness and affect, the commitments which kin make to each other *within families*. Furthermore, like kin relationships, community pressures can reinforce the jajmani tie and thereby help assure its preservation.

Taken together, these kin-like properties of the jajmani system maximize the probabilities that the division of labor necessary to the ritual continuity of the Twice Born castes and the functional integration of the village community can be preserved. All parties concerned both give to the system and derive from it a host of crucial benefits on a diffuse, face-to-face basis which reproduces the solidarities and securities afforded by the kinship system; this renders the jajmani system as meaningful as it can be from the villagers' point of view.

III

Against the background of the foregoing, let us next examine some of the structural features of the jajmani system as revealed in the data from Sherupur.

Regarding the "considerations" which are to Wiser of such fundamental importance, seventeen are listed in his book (1936, pp. 10-11). I reproduce them here because they correspond with my own findings in Sherupur and because they help to illustrate the highly particularistic nature of jajmani ties:

1. Free residence site;
2. Free food for family;
3. Free clothing;
4. Free food for animals;
5. Free timber;

6. Free dung;
7. Rent-free land;
8. Credit facilities,
9. Opportunity for supplementary employment;
10. Free use of tools, implements and draft animals;
11. Free use of raw materials;
12. Free hides;
13. Free funeral pyre lot;
14. Casual leave;
15. Aid in litigation;
16. Variety in diet;
17. Healthful location

In addition to the above there are the formal rates which *jajmans* (patrons) establish with their *kam karnewalas*. These involve agreements by *jajmans* to provide a certain quantity of their grain every six months to their respective *purjans* in accordance with some relevant criterion of amount of service rendered. The following rates were found to be operative in Sherupur:

1. Washerman (*Dhobi*). . . . . . 8 pounds of grain per woman in the household per six months.
2. Blacksmith (*Lohar*). . . . . . 16 pounds of grain per plow owned by *jajman* per six months.
3. Barber (*Nai*). . . . . . . 16 pounds of grain per nuclear unit with child in joint-family per six months.
4. Potter (*Kumhar*). . . . . . . 16 pounds of grain per family per six months.
5. Plowman (*Kori*). . . . . . . 28 pounds of grain per six months plus $2 per month per *jajman*.
6. Priest (*Brahman*) . . . . . . 28 pounds of grain per family at plowing time to compensate for organisms killed by the plow.

There are other avenues of distribution besides the formal reimbursements and the "considerations." High caste families give extra amounts of grain or other crops, like peas, plus balls of molasses (*gur*) and sweatmeats, etc., to their *purjans* at times of marital or funerary rites or after a bountiful harvest. There is no formal rate that can be calculated for these emoluments, however. Cast-off clothing may be given to *purjans* and the head of a Rajput (Kshatriya) landed family in Sherupur indicated the following forms of largesse as being regularly received by the Brahman priest:

1. Fourteen sears (28 lbs.) of grain at plowing time as recompense for the killing of organisms by one's plow.
2. Ten percent of the dowry of any marriage which he helps arrange.
3. Twelve free meals annually (one each month) after there has been a death in the family.
4. One dhoti, one blouse, and one pair of chappals when a woman of the family dies.
5. One dhoti, one shirt, and one pair of chappals when a man in the family dies.
6. One pice to three annas each time an astrological reading is solicited.

A *jajman* and his *purjans* tend to comprise a closed system of socioeconomic interaction in many respects. The barber who cuts his Kshatriya patron's hair may also cut the hair of some of his fellow *purjans* and in exchange receive the services which they are qualified to render. In factional rivalries in villages the intercaste lines that get drawn will often reflect *jajman-purjan* networks. But there are important respects in which *jajmani* relationships are not closed systems of interaction. *Purjans* usually have several Twice Born "clients" and their circuits among their *jajmans* constitute avenues of interfactional communication through which marital negotiations can be conducted and through which ameliorative gestures can be made if rivalries have disrupted pathways of direct approach between families, etc.

Take the case of the barber who was a *purjan* of Sherupur's leading Rajput family. It may be seen in Table 1 that this man serves four villages and a total of fifteen joint-families.

TABLE 1

The Grain Income from the Jajmani Ties of a Barber Serving Sherupur

Village	Joint-Families	Nuclear Units with Children	Amt. of Grain per year
A	2	3	96
B	3	6	192
C	6	11	176
D	4	5	160
Totals	15	25	624

These fifteen joint-families contain twenty-five nuclear units with children, which is the barber's rate-standard, with the result that his yearly grain income from his various *jajmans* is in excess of six hundred pounds. The kind of grain is never stipulated in these arrangements but depends upon the individual agreements arrived at between the parties. The barber's functions and reimbursements do not end here. He cuts hair on a commercial basis besides and averages about thirty dollars a month from this source. He performs a number of additional non-economic services for his patrons. As Opler and Singh (1948, p. 480) put it, "one of his major functions is to groom the living and the dead, and that grooming has special meaning for Hindu ceremonial life, especially in the rites of birth, marriage, and death." In marriage negotiations the *Nai* (barber) is often responsible for garnering information about the status and resources of a potential bride's family. In other words, his interfactional mobility is employed for "marital reconaissance."

After a bride joins her husband it is frequently the *Nai's* wife who is brought in to aid the young woman in her difficult adjustment to her affinal household. Both Opler and Singh (1948) and I found barbers' wives performing this role.

Thus, on the whole, the barber is as indispensable in his way to an orthodox Hindu home as is a son. Relations are close, essential and enduring. To varying degrees, but always to an important degree, this is true of most *jajman-purjan* ties. They involve, as has been said, projections of kinship values into economic relationships which thereby make the latter seem to be "real," i.e., dependable. The villager neither understands nor trusts the "professional" relationship characteristic of the urban-secular society. To him the man who avoids assuming a host of diffuse obligations along with the specific one for which two people have come together at any given moment, i.e., the man who declines to put himself under the obligational structure customary between kin, is thought to be dishonest, capable of feeling no moral compunction to fulfill his side of a bargain. As Marriott (1955, p. 249) declares:

> The people of Kishan Garhi* thus recognize three great social realms—that of kinship and family, which is an area controlled by limitless demands and mutual trust; that of the village and caste, which is an area in part controlled by particular obligations and formal respect; and that of the outside world, of government and the market place, which is an area controlable only by money and power—things which the villager scarcely possesses.

IV

The question of the full amount of goods and services which get circulated by a complete network of *jajman-purjan* ties cannot be answered with the degree of precision possible where pecuniary standards of measurement exist. However, some idea of the volume of grain disseminated by *jajmans* to their *purjans* on the basis of the formal commitments made between them for the village of Sherupur is obtainable. This is simply a matter of calculating the number of service ties of each category known to exist for Sherupur and multiplying by the appropriate rate of re-imbursement in each case. The figures thus obtained are naturally somewhat idealized inasmuch as they do not take cognizance of "considerations" and of innumerable other "intangibles" which are the added hallmarks of this particularistic system of relationships. But they do suggest the magnitude of the economic interaction involved. Table 2 summarizes this aspect of the analysis:

---

*Kishan Garhi is the name of the village which Marriott studied.

TABLE 2

Distributions of Grain to Purjans by their
Jajmans in Sherupur, per annum

Purjans	Units of Reimbursement	Amount of Grain Exchanged (lbs)
Barber (Nai)	23	368
Washerman (Dhobi)	43	688
Blacksmith (Lohar)	18	606
Plowman (Kori)	11	616
Potter (Kumhar)	18	576
Priest (Pundit)	11	616
Carpenter (Barhai)	19	608
Totals:	143	4078

It will be seen that a turn-over of more than two tons of grain a year is attained by the formal jajmani commitments alone in Sherupur. This takes place in a community numbering forty-three families, with a total of two-hundred twenty-eight people, of which only nineteen families function as *jajmans* in any meaningful sense, i.e., as patrons who receive services and disburse grain.

On the other hand, no village is ordinarily self-contained with respect to jajmani relationships. The unit of self-sufficiency is the "local culture." This encompasses the radius of ten or twelve miles within which the bulk of a village's affinal ties are to be found (village exogamy is obligatory in India). Sherupur contains families of blacksmiths, plowmen, tailors, and leatherworkers to serve its nineteen cultivating families. It also has a single resident Brahman priest. But barbers, carpenters, washermen, potters and others come from neighboring communities within the "local culture."

Thus the "local culture" is not only interlaced with affinal connections but also with caste and jajmani ties. It is a kinship of villages founded upon real and quasi-kinship ties among its residents made necessary by the counterpressures of corporate family life, occupational differentiation, ritual avoidance, on the one hand, and the requirements of functional integration of community life, on the other.

V

Although the subject has been dealt with briefly, it is hoped that enough has been said to indicate the basic features and implications of the Hindu Jajmani System. First, we noted that it is a response to certain structural dilemmas posed by rural Hindu society. The Caste System differentiates people into endogamous clusters of joint-families in terms of occupational specialization and standards of differential ritual purity. The net effect of this is to make attitudes of social avoidance a major aspect of village life. But the requirements of community living, especially where there is an advanced division of labor, are that a certain degree of functional integration be achieved and maintained. To accomplish this at the economic level an institutionalized set of procedures exist which facilitate exchanges of goods and services without violating the connubial, commensal, and occupational exclusiveness of caste.

Second, it has been observed that the kinship unit is the principal locus of interaction for the individual; that this unit is the hub of both instrumental and expressive behavior in the village community; and that, consequently, the particularistic values inherent in this structure are to the peasant the most meaningful basis upon which he feels he can establish any type of social relationship. Thus, the Jajmani System is a particularistic set of relationships established between families of different ritual-occupational status which affords assurance of indefinite durability, stable provision of essential services, and observance of a host of kin-like diffuse obligations. In short, jajmani ties interrelate families in a manner comparable to the way in which kinship ties interrelate the members of a family.

The Jajmani System in Sherupur reveals *jajman-purjan* ties set in terms of certain quantities of grain per six months for the particular service being rendered. Unit criteria of reimbursement vary with the nature of the service. Less tangible "considerations" also figure in the pattern of payments and are felt by Wiser (1936) to be more important to the system's maintenance than are the formal rates.

Jajman-purjan networks are not confined within a given village but radiate into the "local culture" (a radius of ten to twelve miles from the village). They take this particular form because no village has a full quota of service castes and must, therefore, utilize appropriate families in nearby villages. Each *purjan* will normally have several *jajmans*. These economic interconnections constitute one of the "local culture's" capillary systems of which affinal connections (born from village exogamy) and caste ties are two others.

The amount of grain turn-over which occurs through the medium of the formal payments made for *purjans*' services in Sherupur exceeds two tons. This takes no account of the numerous informal "considerations" which cannot be easily evaluated. It suggests that for villages like Sherupur, the Jajmani System is a highly significant force in the social and economic life of the people.

BIBLIOGRAPHY

Davis, Kingsley
   1951 The Population of India and Pakistan. Princeton, Princeton University Press.
Embree, John
   1946 Suye Mura: A Japanese Village. London, Kegan Paul.
Firth, Raymond
   1946 Malay Fishing Village. London, Kegan Paul.
   1952 Elements of Social Organization. London, Watts & Co.
Foster, George. M.
   1953 "What is Folk Culture," American Anthropologist, 55: 159-173.
Hutton, J.H.
   1946 Caste in India. Bombay, Oxford Cumberledge Press.
Ishino, Iwao
   1955 "*Oyabun-Kobun*: A Japanese Ritual Kinship Institution," American Anthropologist, 55: 695-707.
Lewis, Oscar
   1951 Life in a Mexican Village: Tepoztian Restudied. Urbana, University of Illinois Press.
   1955 "Peasant Culture in India and Mexico: A Comparative Analysis," in Marriott, McKim, ed., Village India, Chicago, University of Chicago Press, pp. 145-170.
   1956 "Aspects of Land Tenure and Economics in a North Indian Village," Economic Development and Cultural Change," IV: 279-302.

Marriott, McKim
  1955 "Western Medicine in Northern India," in Paul, Benjamin D,, ed , Health, Culture and Community. New York, Russel Sage Foundation, pp. 239-268.
Opler, Morris and Rudra Datt Singh
  1948 "The Division of Labor in an Indian Village," in Coon, Carlton S., ed., A Reader in General Anthropology, New York, Henry Holt & Co., pp. 464-496.
Passin, Herbert
  1955 "Untouchability in the Far East" Monumenta Nipponica (Tokyo) XI: 27-47.
Redfield, Robert Park
  1930 Tepotztian. Chicago, University of Chicago Press.
  1941 The Folk Culture of Yucatan. Chicago, University of Chicago Press.
  1950 Chan Kom Revisited. Chicago, University of Chicago Press.
  1953 The Primitive World and its Transformations. Chicago, University of Chicago Press.
  1955 The Little Community. Chicago, University of Chicago Press.
  1956 Peasant Society and Culture. Chicago, University of Chicago Press.
Wiser, William
  1936 The Hindu Jajmani System. Lucknow, Lucknow Publishing House.
Wolf, Eric R.
  1955 "Types of Latin American Peasantry. A Preliminary Disccussion," American Anthropologist, 57: 452-471.

6

A Jajmani System of North India: Its Structure, Magnitude and Meaning[1]

This essay will examine the economic interaction in rural India which, since the first truly sociological study of it by Wiser (1936), is commonly referred to as the jajmani system. The reasons for this inquiry are threefold. First, there has been a recent spate of discussions of the jajmani system (Kolenda 1963; Pocock 1963; Beidelman 1959; Berreman 1962; Orenstein 1962; Harper 1959; Rowe 1963; Bennett and Despres 1960) which have awakened a great deal of new interest in the system. Second, there has been a constant call by those who deal with economic interaction in Indian villages for detailed substantive data on such interaction in specific localities. Third, the data which form the basis of this study raise at least three issues which in their own right should interest other scholars. These are: (a) the types of relationships and reimbursements which a jajmani system actually involves; (b) the kind of ecological unit that is appropriate for a study of economic interaction in rural India; (c) the relative magnitude of traditional economic interaction in India. The latter is especially important because it bears upon the question of the true meaning of jajman status in Indian social life.

I

The village upon which this discussion will focus has been given the pseudonym of Sherupur. It is situated in a densely populated region south of the city of Faizabad (population 87,000), the capital of Faizabad District. This district lies in the eastern portion of Uttar Pradesh, the largest province in India. Sherupur's corporate limits actually contain five hamlets (*purwah*) with a total population of 750 subdivided into fifteen endogamous, named castes. Two of the five hamlets, the main one which bears the incorporated village's name and another called Naktipur, are binary in nature in the sense that they are close together physically, their residents maintain much mutual interaction, and they are bound together by certain common ceremonial activities. The other three hamlets are widely separated from these two and from each other and therefore possess rather distinct identities. It is to the binary unit, Sherupur-Naktipur, that the data presented in the paper primarily refer. The number of households residing in each hamlet is presented, by caste, in Table 1.

TABLE 1

Distribution of Domestic Groups by Caste Among Sherupur's Hamlets

Caste	Households	Sherupur	Naktipur	Sahjadpur	Jeetpur	Mahmudpur
Brahman	4	3	—	—	—	1
Thakur	7	5	1	—	1	—
Kayastha	2	2	—	—	—	—
Ahir*	46	6	—	18	15	7
Kurmi	26	—	21	—	—	5
Murau	3	3	—	—	—	—
Lohar	2	1	1	—	—	—
Sonar	1	—	1	—	—	—
Darzi**	2	2	—	—	—	—
Gadariya	1	—	1	—	—	—
Kahar	1	1	—	—	—	—
Nai	1	—	—	—	—	—
Teli	1	—	—	—	—	—
Kori	19	18	—	—	—	1
Chamar	3	3	—	—	—	—
TOTAL	119	44	25	18	16	14

*Estimated in part because of refusal to supply me with information in the belief that I was a spy for the taxation department.

**Both households are Muslims.

A JAJMANI SYSTEM: STRUCTURE, MAGNITUDE & MEANING 151

It is clear that the binary unit, Sherupur-Naktipur, is the only one which possesses a high measure of internal social differentiation. Of the fifteen castes found within the incorporated village, thirteen are represented here, whereas none of the other three hamlets has more than four. This unevenness of caste distribution is typical of the area.

II

Wiser (1936) conceptualized the systemic nature of economic relationships in Indian villages in the following words:

> Each caste in the village at some time during the year is expected to render a fixed type of service to each other caste (p. xviii).

> In return for the various services rendered, there are payments in cash and kind made daily, monthly, biyearly, per piece work, and on special occasions, depending on the type of service rendered and in part on the good will of the jajman (p. xxiv)

Wiser was not, however, the first to be aware of a distinctive pattern of economic life in rural India. Among his predecessors, Baden-Powell (1896: 16-17), for example, declared:

> This custom of paying the artisans and menials by allowances of grain (taken out before the division of the crop between the King's officers and the cultivators) is very ancient. It is found in every province, either accompanied by a small grant of land or as the sole allowance. So various are the modes of payments that I can select only one or two characteristic examples. . . . The villagers supply the materials for the work to be done, but do not pay for the labor; a stranger getting a job done would pay for both. The list of artisans varies in different parts, though of course some, being indispensable, are found in all cases, such as blacksmith, potter, shoemaker or cobbler, carpenter, washerman, sweeper, and a barber who is also a

surgeon, and is the proper person to carry messages connected with negotiations for betrothals.

Moreland (n.d.: 160-161) in his study of the Muslim agrarian system also alludes to the jajmani system:

> At the opening of the nineteenth century an ordinary village in the Ceded and Conquered Provinces might be expected to contain, in addition to the peasants engaged in cultivation, three classes of inhabitant, landless laborers, village servants and recipients of charity. The class of landless laborers was, and still is widely spread, and of great economic importance, but, being landless, these men lie outside the scope of the present discussion, and it must suffice to say that, so far as it is possible to judge, they were rarely free, and scarcely ever slaves; they may perhaps be regarded as in a state of rather mild serfdom, the incidents of which varied within wide limits. The village servants were remunerated by methods which bear the stamp of antiquity. They usually had a claim on the peasant's crops, assessed sometimes on the sown area, sometimes on the produce gathered, sometimes on the plow, the oldest unit recognized in the industry. Their claims were sometimes in cash, but more usually in produce; and, apart from the seasonal or annual dues, many of them were allowed to cultivate small portions of village lands; retaining the entire produce for themselves.

The main characteristics of the economic services which Wiser included in the jajmani system were that they were fixed in type, were rendered by one caste to another and involved primarily and characteristically payments in kind although cash payments might also be made under some circumstances.

In Sherupur and Naktipur today there is a division of labor which conforms in general to Wiser's definition of a jajmani system. The following list presents some of the main economic services rendered by and for households in the binary hamlets together with the name of the caste rendering the service and an indication of whether or not the caste is performing its traditional occupation:

A JAJMANI SYSTEM: STRUCTURE, MAGNITUDE & MEANING 153

Type of Economic Service	Caste Rendering the Service	Caste's Traditional Occupation
Barber	Nai (Hindu and Muslim)	Same as today
Blacksmith	Lohar	Same as today
Carpenter	Barhai	Same as today
Cowherd	Ahir	Same as today
Dairyman	Ahir	Same as today
Drummer	Muslim	Non-Hindu
Field laborer	Kori	Cotton weaver
Goldsmith	Sonar	Same as today
Midwife	Chamar	Same as today
	Kori	Cotton weaver
Oil presser	Teli	Same as today
Plowman (Harwar)	Kori	Cotton weaver
Potter	Kumhar	Same as today
Priest	Brahman	Same as today
Scavenger	Kori	Cotton weaver
	Chamar	Same as today
Sweeper (Bhangi)	Kori	Cotton weaver
Tailor	Darzi (Muslim)	Non-Hindu
Washerman	Dhobi	Same as today
Water carrier	Kahar	Same as today

The above list reveals that some castes are associated with specialized activities that are not consonant with their classical assignments in the caste system. Thus the Kori are a weaver caste, but in the contemporary social order none of its members practices this profession because industrialization has defunctionalized them. Instead they are serving as plowmen (Harwar), as landless laborers, as sweepers, as scavengers, and (the women) as midwives (Dai). In their latter two capacities they are performing occupations traditionally associated with the Chamar or leatherworking caste; in fact, in the eyes of the other castes in Sherupur and Naktipur, they are deemed entirely interchangeable with the latter. None of the three permanently resident Brahman households follows the priestly profession today,[2] and the Thakur, as warrior specialists, have lost their traditional caste occupation completely for obvious reasons. Shifts of this kind are commonly observed throughout rural India and in some cases have proved to be extreme. For example, in Totagadde, a village in Mysore State (south India) studied by Harper (1959), carpenter and blacksmith services are performed by a single caste, the Badiga.

Perhaps the most striking development in Sherupur-Naktipur has been the assumption of caste occupations by subgroups of Muslims. Some function as tailors (Darzi). Others are barbers (Nai) and drummers, both of which occupations are ritually important to the Hindu ceremonial pattern. One Muslim barber, Wali Muhammad, has a large clientele in Sherupur and Naktipur that includes several of the most prominent Hindu families.

It is mainly in the most recent studies of the jajmani system that the need for better classifying the types of economic interaction which occur in Indian villages has been emphasized. Harper (1959) and Berreman (1962) deserve credit for being among the first to demonstrate this empirically. Others (Rowe 1963; Kolenda 1963; Gould 1958) have hinted at the need. Pocock, having earlier (Pocock 1958:43) called for a re-examination of the term "hereditary specialization" because the "number of castes in any one area whose 'nature' it is to be ritual specialists under the rubric of pure and impure occupations is relatively few," has now written an extensive essay (Pocock 1963) expanding considerably upon this view. Two significant passages may be quoted:

> I should prefer to say that true specialization for certain important castes derives from the basic opposition of purity and impurity and only by extension of this idea can other castes be said to be "specialized" (p. 82).
> I would suggest that the heterogeneity of service justifies us in distinguishing one category of specialists whose specialization derives from the exigencies of the caste system and not from economic needs or from the intricacy of a craft... The second category, I suggest, emerges initially from the distinction between those who provide a [religious] service and those who provide a commodity and are correctly described as artisans (p. 85).

From an empirical point of view, Harper and Berreman provide a clearer point of departure than Pocock. Berreman (1962:388) found at least four different kinds of economic interaction in the Pahari village which he studied. "When Sirkanda villagers use the term 'jajmans' they refer to one kind of exchange: that of the Brahmin's ritual services to his clients (jajmans) in exchange for 'gifts' paid in grain and other goods." They also apply the term, though not explicitly, "to the traditional arrangement whereby an artisan serves the needs of an agriculturalist in his speciality." Berreman (1962:389) continues:

> In this relationship the artisan or service caste member is paid a fixed portion of grain at each harvest, the amount depending upon the size of the household or landholding of the agriculturalist and the type of service performed. Application of the term "jajman" to the clients of artisans appears to be the result of substitution by analogy of a term which is convenient for explanatory purposes because it is understood by those accustomed to the Brahmanical system of client relationships.

In addition, services are performed in Sirkanda among artisans on a reciprocal basis. According to Berreman (1962: 389), "this is not usually included in either the term 'jajman' or gaikh (the Pahari term for 'jajman') by the villagers." Finally, there are services which are performed on a piecework basis or a daily-wage basis, payments being made in either cash or kind.

Harper (1959) sees economic interaction as being divided into two over-all systems—the Malnad system and the jajmani system. The distinction is basically between economic relations that hinge upon a purely cash crop (in this case, the areca nut) and those that hinge upon the satisfaction of traditional economic needs. The former involve money wages on an open-market basis and arise from the fact that "Malnad villages do not approach economic selfsufficiency."

How well do these findings apply to Sherupur and Naktipur? In general, they fit the situation reasonably well. Here, too, the term jajman applies ultimately to the relationship between a Brahman priest and his clientele and by analogy to artisans of certain kinds. Economic relations are also to be found which fall almost entirely outside the traditional orbit, the more extreme of these being associated with a major cash crop, sugar cane.

Payments for the services of traditional specialists take four principal forms in Sherupur-Naktipur. First is the payment of an agreed amount of grain every six months to a specialist who has been engaged on a permanent basis.[3] Second is the payment of cash or grain on a piecework basis to a specialist who has been engaged on a permanent basis; this is a most important category which has not hitherto been systematically recognized. Third are the exchanges of services which artisans in particular undertake reciprocally and to which Berreman and Rowe have rightly called attention. Finally, there are payments of cash or grain, or both, on piecework basis to any specialist who happens to be handy and is willing to provide a particular service.

Regular and systematic payments to specialists are confined to a total of six castes in Sherupur-Naktipur today: washerman (Dhobi), barbers (Nai), blacksmiths (Lohar), carpenters (Barhai), potters (Kumhar), and plowmen (Harwar of the Kori caste). Actually, only the first four of these groups of specialists receive payments in the form of grain in fixed amounts at the semi-annual harvests in a really significant number of cases. The Harwar are normally rewarded by a combination of free meals, money, and small grants of land, and the potter has only a few permanent clients on this basis, most of them paying him on a permanent piecework basis. Thus what has been conceived of as the ideal traditional economic relationship between a Hindu household and caste specialists is limited in Sherupur and Naktipur to a very small proportion of the entire spectrum of specialists.

The realm within which classical economic relationships operate today probably reflects the changes that have been taking place in Indian society. Early European accounts indicate a far greater number of castes involved in fixed ties rooted in semiannual grain payments, as does Wiser (1936), whose study was done in the early 1930s. However, Jaffri (1935), in two case studies presented in an appendix, gives enough information to suggest that the pattern of reimbursement in eastern

A JAJMANI SYSTEM: STRUCTURE, MAGNITUDE & MEANING   157

Uttar Pradesh 35 years ago was not fundamentally different in kind and in magnitude from what it is today. He nevertheless lists the water carrier (Kahar), tailor (Darzi), village watchman (Chowkidar), and less clearly the cowherd (Ahir) as recipients of fixed semiannual grain payments.

The pattern of payments made by households in Sherupur and Naktipur to the five specialists who are in any measure still implicated in fixed client-patron relationships reimbursed by semiannual grain payments is summarized in Table 2. The grain payments were compiled through direct inquiry at each individual household and were not estimated by multiplying indealized rates by the number of households being served. People were asked to name the specialists with whom they dealt, the basis on which they dealt with them, and the amounts and kinds of payments they were making at the time. Idealized rates were ascertained, of course, for comparative purposes, but it was found that such rates, taken alone, can be highly misleading. What a specialist tells you he charges, multiplied by the number of households he serves, will yield an ideal figure for his income from rendering traditional services, but this may differ widely from the sum arrived at by approaching each of his clients directly and totaling the amounts they report they have actually paid at the last two or three harvests.

TABLE 2

Types of Reimbursements and Amounts of Grain Payments Made by Jajmans in Sherupur and Naktipur to Five Sets of Specialists

Category of Specialist	No. Grain Payments	Pounds per Year	Average lbs. per Year	No. of Barter Payments	Money to Specific Specialist	Money to Available Specialist	Total No. of Relationships
Dhobi	54 (77%)	1,679	31.1	4 (6%)	5 (7%)	7 (10%)	70
Nai	43 (62%)	1,238	26.5	5 (7%)	7 (10%)	15 (21%)	70
Lohar	46 (67%)	1,872	40.7	4 (6%)	8 (12%)	10 (15%)	68
Barhai	48 (69%)	1,967	41.0	5 (7%)	4 (6%)	12 (18%)	69
Kumhar	5 (7%)	114	22.8	5 (7%)	52 (74%)	8 (12%)	70
Total	196 (57%)	6,870	35.1	23 (7%)	76 (22%)	52 (14%)	347

Among the five specialists considered, the washermen (Dhobi) are most frequently retained on a fixed, grain-payment basis, i.e., by 77 per cent of their clientele at an average reimbursement of 31.1 pounds of grain. This is, at least in part, associated with the fact that washing clothes is deemed very defiling and is, therefore, particularly directly implicated in the pure-impure dichotomy which is a central preoccupation of Hindu religious orthodoxy.

The services of carpenters (Barhai) and blacksmiths (Lohar) are the next most frequently sought on the fully traditional basis and are by far the most highly rewarded on the average. I think this arises from a combination of two facts. On the one hand, carpenters and blacksmiths play central skilled roles in the maintenance of household and agricultural equipment at a time when agricultural production, under the impetus of deliberate government stimulation, is growing ever more lucrative and economically important. On the other hand—a fact not unrelated to the foregoing—the capacity to retain traditional ties with carpenters and blacksmiths marks a household as socially important. Their retention is connected with what I would call "social orthodoxy" in order to emphasize the interconnectedness of the religious and social components of status in the minds of most Hindus.

The barbers (Nai) are lower in their quantitative importance than the three specialists previously considered because, I think, their strictly economic significance has been declining rapidly as a result of the cheapness and availability of the razor blade and the comparative lucrativeness of commercial barbering. It is because the ritual importance of the barbers still exceeds that of the other specialists here considered that their occupation remains in the same class as the others even in the degree that it does.

The potters (Kumhar) are clearly a survival. Only 7 per cent of their economic interaction is of the traditional kind. Their work is conducted nowadays almost entirely on a piece-work basis because commercialism has deeply penetrated ceramics manufacturing and because the specificity of an item of pottery makes it easily translatable into pecuniary terms. What is significant about the potters who serve Sherupur and Naktipur is that they tend to retain a client-patron type of relationship with particular households even though the commodities they supply are paid for piecemeal.

Differential resort to the four types of economic relationships which may exist between users and renderers of specialized services clearly reflects hierarchical considerations, and a definite pattern emerges when households are ordered according to such considerations. I have adopted a hierarchical classification which is broadly functional and at the same time reflects gradations in material condition and ritual purity. It divides all the castes in the jajmani system into four categories. In the first category I have placed the Brahman and Thakur castes and have labeled them Elite-Pure because traditionally they have occupied the apex of the intermeshed religious, political, and economic hierarchy in Sherupur and its region. In the lowest category I have placed the Kori (weaver) and Chamar (leatherworker and scavenger) castes and have called them Menial Impure because they have traditionally occupied the lowest position in the hierarchy.

In the middle fall two other categories which have traditionally occupied an intermediate position—neither pure nor impure, neither rich nor poor. These are primarily the castes which live directly by cultivating the soil and practicing animal husbandry and those which perform specialized craft and craft-like services to households and farming operations. In very general terms, the Agriculturalist category probably slightly outranks the Artisan category in material and ritual status, enjoying a better material status because of the comparative prosperity of agriculture and a better ritual status because their occupations is "caste free" (cf. note 7). The Agricultural category embraces the Ahir (farmers and dairymen), Kurmi (farmers), Murau (vegetable cultivators and regular cultivators), Gadariya (traditionally goatherds but farmers today), and Kayastha (traditionally accountants but also farmers today). The Artisan category includes the Sonar (traditionally goldsmiths but also ironsmiths today), Lohar (ironsmiths), Darzi (tailors), and Kahar (traditionally water carriers but shopkeepers in Sherupur-Naktipur today). Table 3 analyzes the services rendered to households of the four categories.

The nine households of Brahman and Thakur comprising the Elite-Pure category maintain the highest proportion (78 per

TABLE 3

Services Rendered by Five Sets of Specialists to 70 Households in Sherupur and Naktipur, by Class

Category of Specialist	No. House-holds	No. Grain Payt's	Pounds Per Year	Average lbs. per Year	No. Barter Payt's	Money to Specific Specialist	Money to Available Specialist	Total No. of Relationships
Elite-Pure	9	35(78%)	1,056	30.2	1(2%)	9(20%)	....	45
Agriculturist	33	111(68%)	4,058	35.6	1(0%)	38(23%)	14(9%)	164
Artisan	7	5(16%)	168	33.6	21(66%)	1(2%)	5(16%)	32
Menial Impure	22	45(43%)	1,558	35.3	....	28(25%)	33(31%)	105
Total	70	196(57%)	6.870	35.1	23(7%)	76(22%)	52(14%)	347

cent) of traditional economic relationships with the five sets of specialists and no relationships that do not retain at least some traditional flavor. The Agriculturist castes are next in order. The Menial-Impure castes are lowest in this regard (43 per cent), and highest in their proportion of entirely unspecific economic ties (5 per cent). The Artisan castes also retain a high measure of traditional economic interaction in the sense that only 16 per cent of their economic ties are altogether unspecific: however, the high concentration of barter services (66 per cent) among them sets them apart from the other categories in a manner which, incidentally, wholly confirms the observations of Berreman, Rowe, and Pocock previously alluded to.

It is important to note that even the Menial-Impure castes maintain traditional economic ties with the five sets of specialists in 43 per cent of their relationships, whereas only 31 per cent of latter fall completely outside the class of fixed ties. This is highly significant when we recall the frequent impression left by other studies of the jaimani system that only high castes act as patrons (jajman) and low castes as clients (purjan, kamin, kam karnewala) and that specialists never accept patrons who are lower in the social and ritual hiererchy than themselves. This view stems, I fear, from the overemphasis placed on the purely economic factors in the jajmani system and from a tendency to draw a fallacious analogy between jajmani relations and "feudal" relations. This matter will be taken up in detail in the last section.

Beidelman (1959) and others (Wiser 1936; Kolenda 1963) have suggested that the exalted status of the elite castes has enabled them to obtain traditional services at lower rates than castes of lower rank. The Sherupur data appear to confirm this, at least as far as average reimbursements are concerned, as well as its corollary, namely, that high-caste specialists are paid more for their services. Among the four castes which still retain a significant number of the most traditional jajmani relationships, as revealed in Table 2, the washermen receive the lowest average remuneration, the barbers next lowest, and the carpenters and blacksmiths the highest—an order of precedence which accords perfectly with their relative traditional statuses.

Several of the less easily quantifiable occupational specializations likewise merit some attention. One is the plowmen (Harwar), who are not really craftsmen but perform, what I call a categorically circumscribed service. All plowmen in Sherupur and Naktipur belong to the Menial-Impure Kori caste and are engaged exclusively by members of the Elite-Pure category. Nine Brahman and Thakur households retain the services of ten Harwar. In nine of these ten cases the plowman is given a small grant of agricultural land, and nine of them receive a meal a day and eight rupees a month. One jajman gives his plowmen land but not the other emoluments, and one gives him the other emoluments but no land. The amount of land involved averages slightly more than one acre per plowman, and the labor required is no more than six months per annum.

The Chamar constitute an important category of specialist in a Hindu community because it is they who traditionally absorb the impurities associated with the removal of dead animals, working with leather products, childbirth, etc. Thus the question "Who is your Chamar," may elicit reference to a household's cobbler, its midwife, or the person who is called upon to dispose of the carcass of a dead animal. In all three instances, the tendency today is to pay for such services more in cash than in kind. The midwife's role has its principal meaning in the ritual context, those of the other two in what I call, somewhat unsatisfactorily, the production context. I can offer no reliable estimate of the amount of money, grain, or other commodities that change hands in connection with these professions.

Another aspect of these roles is their "attributional" character (see Marriott 1959). Apparently a "Chamar" is what a "Chamar" does. When I asked respondents whom they retained as Chamar, they would give the name of an individual whom they engaged in this capacity. Although always of the Menial-Impure category, this individual might be either a Kori or a Chamar, despite the fact that these two castes consider themselves absolutely distinct. The Kori, in fact, deem themselves ritually superior to the Chamar, whose name connotes unclean status in the community, whereas they associate their own caste name with the honorable profession of weaving, even though no member of the caste weaves for a living today. What we apparently have here is an instance of the "Chamarization" of a caste, i.e., a case where a caste has been progressively forced by necessity to perform the most defiling occupations simply because their old caste occupation, with its low but defiled status, evaporated with the onset of industrialization.

The small number of actual Chamar households in the village and its vicinity has doubtless contributed to this process. Most of the scavengers in Sherupur and Naktipur are Kori. The three Chamar households continue to practice shoemaking and midwifery, but they dislike scavenging and have helped to withdraw from this highly polluting occupation through their identification with the so-called Raidasi movement, which endeavors to improve the lot of Chamar everywhere within the Hindu cosmos by adhering to the doctrines of Ravi Das, a saint of the Indian Middle Ages. It seems to matter little to a jajman who does his "Chamar" work for him so long as it is performed We see here an illustration of the "functional interchangeability" which Kolenda (1963) considers a general attribute of jajmani systems: "As one compares village complements of services, it is striking that where a specialist caste is absent, the caste's function is often provided by some other caste." In my view, such functional interchangeability is a necessary attribute of an ongoing jajmani system, particularly with respect to impure occupations, for a "clean" household cannot, by definition, retain its "clean" status unless certain kinds of work and ritual procedures with impure implications are transferred to others. If the traditional absorber of a specific form of impurity is not available, then the power and persuasion of the "clean" household must be employed to uncover someone else who will function as a substitute.

In the ritual context, the barber (Nai), as is well known, performs numerous religiously meaningful duties at birth, marriage, and death ceremonies, to name only the most important ones. His role is nicely summed up by Opler and Singh (1948) when they characterize him as the one who "grooms the living and the dead." He derives his income in substantial measure from semiannual grain disbursements as we have seen, but for his work at ceremonies he receives additional gifts of money, grain, clothing, etc. which vary according to the occasion, the means, and the inclination of the jajman. The Brahman priest, on the other hand, derives all his income from his religious functions, which are manifold. In addition to being called upon to participate in rites of passage, the Pandit provides astrological readings and conducts special rites like those held when a smallpox epidemic threatens.[4] For such specialized services he receives a wide variety of emoluments. They have not been calculated for this study because, as in the case of the Chamar midwife and others whose services are mainly ritual, they cannot be objectified as can the payments to the five grain-receiving specialists.

It is a characteristic of the ritual context of the jajmani system that reimbursements depend heavily on the particular rite, its particular occasion, and the particular household. The rituals of a particular household express both its individual character and the structure of Hinduism in general. The two are integrally intertwined in Indian religion; the ritual specialist, particularly the priest, gives simultaneous expression to both. God, man, the priesthood, the sacramentalized social order, and the kinship system converge in a ceremony which ritualizes a particular event in a household even whose everyday activities are seen as ultimately expressive of religion.

Sweepers and field laborers are also important functionaries in Sherupur and Naktipur. Technically, sweeping is supposed to be done by the Bhangi caste. Since no representatives of this defiled caste are found in the area, however, the task is performed by some of the Kori—yet another instance of "functional interchangeability."

Field labor is, of course, a crucial economic requirement, especially at harvest time. This work is usually reimbursed at the rate of four to eight annas (five to ten cents) a day plus the right to a certain amount of gleanings from the harvested crops. Although Hindu tradition does not specify field labor as the province of any particular caste, it is nevertheless regarded as menial work becoming only to those of unclean status, and it has consequently come to be associated in the main with members of the Kori caste. Besides the poverty and the defiled status of the Kori, their sheer numerical abundance renders them available as a source of recruitment for every kind of demeaning work. Their eighteen domestic groups provide a reservoir of 25 males and 45 females between the ages of twelve and fifty, augmented by 33 older and younger members who are available on a part-time basis.

Two Muslim households serve as tailors (Darzi), receiving a variety of goods and cash for their important services. Their clientele is confined almost exclusively to the binary hamlets. Masons (Mistri), usually either Kori or members of one of the agricultural castes, move about the locality selling their skills for about two rupees a day. Dairymen (Ahir) also engage in agriculture. Milk is dispensed on a strictly cash basis to whoever is willing to pay the price. The cost is eight annas a seer (two pounds). It is rare today to engage an Ahir to tend a herd of cows on anything other than a cash basis. It is still rarer to engage a Kahar (water carrier) on any basis except in the ritual context. Another occupation for which traditional forms of economic interaction have disappeared is that of the oil presser (Teli). He still does a brisk business, but it is entirely on a cash basis.

We may now inquire briefly into the manner of engaging specialists. A commonly held view is that jajmani ties, once established, are inherited agnatically by both parties and that upon the partition of joint families clients are subdivided among coparceners in the same manner as other property. Although my data are not sufficiently complete to deal with all aspects

of the establishment and temporal continuity of jajmani relationships, some comments are possible concerning particularly the extent to which caste and kinship affect their perpetuation.

To some extent, these ties are indeed inherited on an agnatic basis. However, the pattern is mixed, and exceptions frequently prove to be as important as the rule. Thakur households, for example, belong to a common agnatic lineage, which in turn belongs to the Surajbans clan.[5] These households do not, however, act in concert with respect to the retention of traditional specialists. One cluster, consisting of Ram Narais Singh, Sukhraj Singh, and Shiv Datt Singh, shares specialists in eight out of nine cases, as is consistent with the fact that they are more closely related to one another than to the other Thakur households. But conflict is also a factor, for they form a faction that is antagonistic toward the other Thakur households led by Ram Babhuti Singh, who represents the senior segment of the lineage. The same households, moreover, are residentially contiguous. One Kayastha household, that of Ram Saran Lal, also retains specialists in common with this Thakur grouping. His house is propinquitous to theirs, and, moreover, he identifies with them by claiming equivalent traditional status, contending that the Kayastha, like the Rajput, are descended from the old Kshatriya varna.

Lal Singh, another Thakur, retains different specialists from all the other Thakur households. He lives in Naktipur, whereas the others reside in Sherupur, and the specialists whom he employs are the same as those engaged by various Kurmi households who are his neighbours in Naktipur. In other words, residential location can sometimes be as important as kinship ties in affecting the choice of specialists.

The correspondence between kinship ties and economic ties is most pronounced where the relationship is of the order of siblings or first cousins, or some combination of the two. Four Ahir households in Sherupur (those of Shankar, Lakhan, Surajbali, and Ram Din) have nearly all of their specialists in common. All are descendants of a common great-grandfather, all live close together as a result of subsequent partitions of the original house site. The house of Ram Din stands at a right angle to those of his kinsmen and consequently faces on a different clearing in the hamlet, along with the residences of an important Chamar (Nankhai), a more distantly related Ahir (Ram Namaj), the Village Level Worker, and some Kori households. Ram Din's carpenter, the only specialist he engages who is different from those engaged by his Ahir kinsmen, is the same man whose services Nankhai Chamar and Ram Namaj Ahir also retain.

The three Murau domestic groups are three generations removed from an original partition of a joint family followed by another partition in the next generation. The three domestic groups resulting from these events reside in adjoining dwellings and have specialists in common in thirteen of fifteen instances. Five Kori households, interconnected by a very complex pattern of kin ties, retain among them eighteen traditional ties (some on a grain-payment and some on fixed-tie but piecework basis) all but one of which are identical Nearly all the Kurmi domestic groups are dispersed among ten groupings which have agnatic ties three generations or less in depth. In each such grouping the tendency to retain the same specialists is pronounced.

Service relationships are commonly inherited. Residential location, however, frequently overrides even tendencies toward homogeneity based on close agnation, as with Ram Din Ahir, and occasionally promotes it in directions divorced altogether from kinship considerations, as with Ram Saran Lal Kayastha and Lal Singh.

III

With very few exceptions, sociological discussions of rural India have invariably made "the village" the prime, where not the exclusive, conceptual focus regardless of what was being concretely discussed. In recent years, some authors (cf. Mukerjee 1961; Mayer 1958, 1960) have begun to question that the village is an appropriate unit for a number of analytical purposes. Although this does not mean that there is universal agreement concerning what alternative units are suitable for rural investigations, it is clear that for many of the problems centering upon caste, kinship, politics, and economics a concept like "local region" or "locality," which embraces a number of village communities, is needed. It proved useful, for example, in my study of the microdemography of marriages (Gould 1960). Mayer (1960) used such an idea in his study of caste and kinship in Malwa, as did Miller (1954) in a study dealing with the political limits of castes in Malabar. Bailey (1958, 1960) has approached politics and economics in Orissa in a similar fashion.

In both anthropology generally and Indian studies in particular earlier scholarship created preconceptions about the village which became hard to criticize and modify because they had been entrenched so long. Foster's (1953) criticism of Redfield's (1944) folk-urban continuum was one of the first attempts to lead anthropological thinking away from an inflexible belief that a peasant village constitutes a conceptual whole of the same kind as a primitive tribe. The village is part of a wider whole, asserted Foster, and can only be understood as a component of a complex society which contains cities as well as villages. In India, Maine (1887) propounded his thesis that the "Aryan community" was the model against which contemporary village conditions might be judged. When Baden-Powell (1896) later disputed Maine's view, it was mainly a disagreement about whether the model should be the undifferentiated Aryan or "joint" village or whether it should be broadened to include at least two types of village—the "joint" and the "raiyatwari" types. There was still, however, no question of disputing the conceptual reality of the village itself. Baden-Powell (1896:3) declared:

> The whole argument of this book is not so much to throw doubt on the general idea of early communial ownership, as to insist on the specific facts of Indian village history, and to the qualified sense in which such collective ownership as is deemed predicable can be asserted.

Wiser, unfortunately, had little of empirical value to go on except his own data. It is not surprising, therefore, that like others of his day, he too postulated the self-contained village as the purest manifestation of intercaste economic interaction and that instances to the contrary must be "corruptions" engendered by the effects of modernization. Consequently, he states (Wiser 1936: xviii):

> Where the village is large enough [sic], the clientele will be limited by the boundaries of the village. If the village is not large or the number of carpenter families are too numerous to meet the needs of one village, the clientele extends to small neighboring villages where there are no carpenters in residence.

Elsewhere (Wiser 1936:110) says:

> Thus we find that the Hindu jajmani system in its purest form [sic] was a corruption [sic] of the ancient system of "the custom of communal ownership" directed by the panchayat.

We can point to Kolenda (1963) as evidence that even among the most sophisticated contemporary thinkers there remains much ambiguity concerning the real conceptual status of the village in Indian rural studies. She seems to assume, and suggests, that many of those whose work she reviews assume, that the acceptance of extra-village clients by specialists results from an imbalance in supply and demand and is, consequently aberrant. Thus she states (Kolenda 1963:47):

> Many observers have mentioned the fact that various kamins serve more than one village or hamlet to supplement their clientele. Oscar Lewis has asked if mobility of kamins between villages in an area is not necessary for the operation of the system.

The word "supplement" reveals her bias, which arises in part because, like the earlier scholars, she confuses hamlet and village and in part because she fails to recognize explicitly that the community is a demographic unit whereas the jajmani system is an economic unit. Identity of the two is neither essential nor normal in rural India.

Let us consider the case of Sherupur. For many purposes it is indeed legitimate to speak of "the village" as the incorporated entity consisting of 750 people dispersed in five hamlets. It is this entity to which the government refers when taxes are assessed and collected, censuses are taken, local or national elections are held, development funds are allocated, school districting and construction are undertaken, co-operative bank offices are built, health districts are established, police business is conducted, etc. In this sense, therefore, Sherupur is a whole. The effects of Sherupur's unity at this level are apparent in the testimony of the villagers themselves.

However, in connection with marriages, this incorporated entity is not the appropriate referent. Caste endogamy remains totally effective in concert with the rule enjoining village exogamy. Thus, respecting marital negotiations and ceremonies, Sherupur means the people of one's own caste who alone are significantly involved in the giving and taking of brides. Furthermore, in such negotiations and ceremonies, it is often castemates in one's own hamlet who are relevant because, in all but the smallest villages, caste members residing here normally comprise the most intimate circle from the standpoint of taking common action. Consequently they tend to see themselves as somewhat distinct even from caste brethren in other hamlets of the same incorporated village. The Ahir of Sherupur proper come mostly from a single descent group and display a high measure of kin solidarity, whereas the majority of Ahir reside in the three outlying hamlets and reveal no close agnatic ties with the former. When Shankar Ahir's daughter of Sherupur proper was married, more people from other castes living in Sherupur attended the wedding than did fellow Ahir from the other hamlets. As a matter of fact, most of the other Ahir attending came from the hamlets of adjoining incorporated villages, such as Masodha, with whom Shankar and his immediate kin enjoy closer social bonds.

With respect to the jajmani system, too, the incorporated village is relatively unimportant. Instead, the relevant unit is a network of economic relationships whose spatial dimensions are defined not by corporate boundaries but by the location of households of specialists and their clienteles (see Map 1). In the binary hamlets of Sherupur and Naktipur, 65 out of 70 households employ at least one specialist from among the five categories of specialists who are reimbursed by payments in cash or kind at each harvest. The total number of persons rendering washerman, barber, blacksmith, carpenter, and potter services to patrons in Sherupur and Naktipur is 35. Two blacksmiths live in the

THE HINDU CASTE SYSTEM

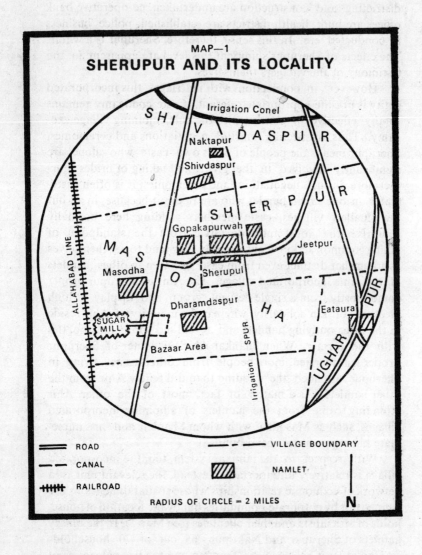

MAP—1
SHERUPUR AND ITS LOCALITY

binary hamlets themselves, and a barber resides in Jeetpur, another hamlet of Sherupur. The rest, however, come from six hamlets situated within the boundaries of four other local incorporated villages. In other words, the need for the services rendered by these five categories of traditional specialists must be met almost entirely on the basis of extravillage economic ties. The village in the corporate sense is by no means a self-contained unit in this respect; on the contrary, in this aspect of their economic life the people of Sherupur and Naktipur are far more directly involved with people in the hamlets of adjoining incorporated villages than they are with those living in the remaining three hamlets of their own village. Table 4 shows the spatial distribution of the individual specialists who serve clients in Sherupur and Naktipur together with the quantity of grain which gets circulated among the hamlets through these specialists' economic activities.

TABLE 4

Location by Village and Hamlet of the Specialists Rendering Traditional Services to the 70 Households of Sherupur and Naktipur

Village and Hamlet	Dhobi	Nai	Lohar	Barhai	Kumhar	Grain Payments (in Pounds)
Sherupur						2,105
Sherupur	—	—	1	—	—	
Naktipur	—	—	1	—	—	
Jeetpur	—	1	—	—	—	
Masodha						2,061
Masodha	—	1	1	—	3	
Gopakapurwah	—	—	—	—	2	
Dharamdaspur	—	—	—	7	—	
Shivdaspur						2,356
Naktipur	13	—	—	—	—	
Shivdaspur	—	4	—	—	—	
Ugharpur						348
Etaura	—	—	—	1	—	
Total	13	6	3	8	5	6,870

An undetermined additional quantity of grain, money, and other commodities is distributed within this local framework as a result of the activities of the less formally reimbursed specialists. In most instances, however, the interaction involved here is confined to persons within the binary hamlets because it concerns mainly the various unclean and menial tasks that are performed by Kori and Chamar or else the ritual services performed by the Brahman priest. In either case the location of the relevant specialist rather than the location of village boundaries is the determining consideration. The Brahman priest illustrates the nature of this order of interaction and the forms which reimbursements may take under such circumstances. In the spring of 1961 this priest conducted a great rite (*puja*) at the shrine of *Bhagoti Mai*, the goddess of smallpox, when an epidemic of this disease broke out in the community. Four annas were collected from every household in Sherupur and Naktipur as payment for this three-day ceremony. This pattern of reimbursement, incidentally, also constitutes evidence in support of our earlier statement that these two hamlets are closely bound together.

There are a number of reasons why a jajmani system cannot normally be entirely contained within the framework of a single village community. The first reason is demographic. Even under modern conditions the number of specialized caste groups participating in such a system is large, with the result that villages which normally contain only a few hundred persons are unlikely to display consistently and uniformly the complex division of labor which the jajmani system presupposes. The unevenness in the distribution of castes can be very striking. Two Kumhar families in Gopakapurwah (Masodha) are the only really large-scale manufacturers of pottery in the locality, with the result that their circle of clients and their volume of cash business are both great. Nearly every household in Sherupur and Naktipur obtains its ceramic articles from these two specialists. The thirteen washermen serving households in the binary hamlets reside in a hamlet of Shivdaspur (Naktipur), which consists almost exclusively of members of the Dhobi caste. Most of the clothing in the locality is washed by washerman from this single hamlet.[6]

Another reason is that specialists tend to expand their clienteles as widely as possible to maximize their incomes. There are no traditional restrictions imposed upon the number or location of the clients a specialist may engage; the only limitation is the practical one of the number of households he is able or inclined to serve. A good illustration of this point is the barber, Wali Muhammad. Although his natal village is Masodha, the largest in the locality (1,200 people), most of Wali Muhammad's patrons are from hamlets of other incorporated villages. Six are from Sherupur proper, seven are from Naktipur, eight are from Korasapurwah, a hamlet of Zamooratganj, and only one is from a hamlet (Kalikapurwah) of Masodha itself.

The vicissitudes of reproductive rates and other factors which affect the availability of caste personnel in a locality from generation to generation are important, especially because to them must be added the further disruption in temporal continuity which disagreements between specialists and their clients engender. If a jajman is unsatisfied with a specialist's work or prices he is frequently compelled to seek a substitute from another hamlet because other caste mates of the man discharged in his own hamlet may refuse to take his place out of loyalty to him.

IV

To date, no serious attempt has been made to ascertain what proportion of a community's wealth actually gets channelized into traditional economic interaction. Everyone who has dealt with the jajmani system has assumed that the main reason for its persistence and popularity has been the economic and exploitative interests of a particular privileged class. Thus I have myself asserted (Gould 1958:429):

Basically the distinction is between the land-owning cultivating castes, on the one hand, who dominate the social order and the landless craft and menial castes, on the other, who are subordinate to them.

Pocock (1963:79) similarly declares:

> ... if two [jajmani] relationships do not constitute a system they do seem to constitute an organization. They are organized around one institution, the dominant caste of a given area.

Beidelman (1959) explicitly equates the jajman with "exploiter" and the specialist with "exploited" and characterizes the system as "feudal." He believes the jajmani system to be one of the chief instruments of coercion, control, and legitimation wielded by highcaste, land-owning Hindus. Orenstein (1962) strongly opposes this view but on somewhat different grounds than are proferred here. If the quantitative importance of the jajmani system and the actual social composition of the jajman "class" in Sherupur and Naktipur are any criteria, these earlier views of traditional economic interaction have seriously oversimplified the situation and are urgently in need of revision.

The 70 domestic groups in Sherupur and Naktipur who are involved in jajmani relationship own 350 of the 500 acres of land cultivated by the entire village. The acreage distribution of crops and yields per acre are recorded by the Village Level Worker in the normal course of his duties. Table 5 summarizes

TABLE 5

Crop Distributions and Yields for 70 Domestic Groups in 1960

Crop	Acres Sown	Yield per Acre		Total Yields in Pounds Food Grains, Sugar Cane and Peas	
		Mounds per Acre	Pounds per Acre		
Wheat	105	18	1,440	151,200	
Rice	105	20	1,600	168,000	
Gram	35	30	2,400	84,000	
Peas	28	15	1,200	33,600	
Barley	3	20	1,600	4,800	
Sugar Cane	70	800	64,000		4,480,000
Total	346*			441,600	4,480,000

*Four additional acres are sown in various minor crops.

the data from this source for the year 1960 on the 70 domestic groups under consideration.

Sugar cane is the most valuable crop in the area because it finds a guaranteed market in the local sugar mill. There is a government price-support program for sugar cane as well as a law requiring cane millers to accept any cane brought to the mill by local growers For this reason, very little sugar cane enters into the pattern of reimbursement for traditional economic services. It thus lies outside the jajmani system, like areca nuts in the case of the Malnad system in Mysore State (Harper 1959). The crop is converted directly into cash and is used for paying taxes, repaying loans, and meeting other cash contingencies.

It is the other crops, mainly food grains and vegetables, that are primarily involved in semiannual payments in kind. The peasants themselves indicate this when they say that they give so much "grain" (*anaj*) to a specialist at harvest time. In gauging the magnitude of payments under the jajmani system, therefore, it is appropriate to make comparisons with the total production of crops other than sugar cane. From harvests relevant to the jajmani system, 441, 600 pounds (221 tons) of grain and peas are obtained in an ordinary year by the 70 domestic groups under consideration. Of this, only 6,870 pounds are disbursed as fixed payments to traditional specialists. How much more grain goes out in less specific payments is uncertain, but I doubt if it amounts to more than an additional ton, and it is probably less. Relative to total grain and pea production, therefore, the amount involved in traditional economic interaction is remarkably small—only 1.5 per cent of the gross harvest. It is thus easy to understand why specialists so often complain that the amount of economic support they are able to derive from the performance of their traditional occupations is insufficient to sustain them and why, consequently, they endeavor to expand both their clientele and their income from other sources wherever possible. It is doubtful whether the situation has ever been essentially different.

Relative to normal agricultural productivity, then, the maintenance of traditional economic relationships is not particularly costly, except in instances of extreme destitution. This is especially true if we do not confine ourselves to the most orthodox manifestations of jajmani, namely, fixed semiannual grain payments, but include as well the circumstantially dictated "compromise" relationships (service exchanges among artisans and fixed services reimbursed on a piecework basis) which form such important parts of traditional economic interaction in Sherupur and Naktipur. Pocock (1963:85) states the matter perfectly:

> Important as are the effects of the introduction of cash payments, the difference amongst these various relationships is not in the nature of the payment. It is rather in the nature of the service.

Under these circumstances, an analysis of the jajmani system which places emphasis on its strictly economic meanings, or which sees it as an essential or key structural component of a "feudal" or some other kind of pre-industrial oligarchic social order, seems unwarranted. The magnitude of the system is small by any measure of economic activity, which implies that "rational" economic motivations can hardly be adduced to account for its persistence.

I suggest that traditional economic interaction persists because, regardless of the economic and political changes that have occurred in India, it continues to be of fundamental importance to the maintenance of the social status and patterns of social interaction that are essential to the successful practice of rural Hinduism. The jajman is not primarily an economically and politically homogeneous class but a religio-economic category uniquely adapted to Indian civilization. The jajman expresses the convergence of the sacred and the secular in rural economic interaction. His existence presupposes the existence of the value system embodied by the Brahman caste. The archetype of the jajman status is apprehended in the complementary relationship between the Brahman priest as ceremonial specialist and his client, or jajman, who is ideally an orthodox, Twice Born householder. In this sense, the jajman status is universal throughout India and is not confined merely to peasant villages, which is the reason why Berreman (1963), Pocock (1963), and Majumdar (1960) have cautioned against using the term without careful qualification. Thus the jajman has never been synonymous with a class in the true sense of the word, even within the highly circumscribed ritual context. An orthodox, Twice Born householder can belong to any of the top three varna (Brahman, Kshatriya, and Vaisya), which are absolutely distinct from each other both ritually and occupationally. Becoming a jajman has never implied any alteration of one's varna. *The bond between all jajmans is enjoyment of a common religio-economic relationship with a Brahman and not enjoyment of a common relationship to the sources of wealth and power in society.*

Similarly, in the context of modern sociological analyses of the jajmani system, assertions that jajman status coincides with a landlord class, a dominant caste, or the like, are equally dubious. In part this misconception has arisen from the overestimation of the purely economic importance of the jajmani system previously alluded to. In addition, however, it has arisen from a failure to realize that the jajman status does not depend upon membership in any particular social group but upon the possession of land, or access to the produce from land by whatever means, and upon *the determination to use one's resources in the practice of social and religious orthodoxy.* Moreover, access to farm land has always been "caste free"[7] in India, according to Mathur (1958) and others (e.g., Pocock 1963; Mayer 1960), which means that the modest means needed to maintain at least some semblance of jajman status has technically always been available to members of any caste in the hierarchy.

Evidence from Sherupur-Naktipur will be marshaled in support of the view that jajman status refers to a religio-economic category rather than a social class. First, we have documented every instance of jajman status relative to the five traditionally reimbursed specialists to learn whether the status does in fact correspond to any sociologically meaningful class. The data are assembled in Table 6. Listed in vertical order are the names of the heads of every household in Sherupur and Naktipur, subdivided by caste. In horizontal order are listed the names of every specialist who provides services on a fixed basis of any kind (whether for grain or cash) to any of the 70 households in the binary hamlets. The households listed in vertical order are jajman to the extent that they are served by any of the specialists listed horizontally. Any caste-specific or class-specific patterns pertaining to jajman status will be revealed in this way if they exist.

There are obviously no such patterns. No class or caste uniformity exists with respect to the retention of specialists. Specialists who serve Brahmans may or may not also serve Thakur, Ahir, Kori, and Chamar. Chhunalal Dhobi, for example, washes clothes for all three Brahman households and also for a Kayastha household, two Ahir households, three Murau households, a Kori household, and a Chamar household. This means that, vis-a-vis Chhunalal Dhobi, common jajman status is shared by households spanning the entire spectrum of ritual purity and the entire range of economic standing. Such a congeries of socially disparate households can hardly constitute a class in any sociological sense. They are alike only in their propensity to maintain a particular religio-economic status, that of jajman.

Another point which emerges from Table 6 is that some persons are both jajman and specialists depending upon the context. That is, they serve some jajman as specialists while themselves functioning as jajman who retain a retinue of specialists. Such circularity makes the jajmani system fundamentally different from a feudal system. In the latter, there are gradations of enfeoffment which cause persons to be simultaneously vassal to a higher ranked noble and lord to a lower ranked vassal, but nobility constitutes a definitely bounded, hierarchically graded class. A situation cannot arise wherein a serf and a noble enjoy indentical rights in the social status system. Yet this is precisely what occurs in the jajmani system.

Let us consider further examples. Tiri Lohar, of Sherupur, has clients for whom he performs ironsmithing services in all but one of the castes, aside from his own, in Sherupur and Naktipur. He is a specialist to three Brahman households, two Chamar households, and many others, all of whom are consequently jajman to him. But he is in turn jajman to the washerman Buddhu and the potter Jhurai. Shivlal, Basante, Antu, and Bipat, all members of the low ranked Kori caste, serve as plowmen to landed Thakur households. Not only are they specialists but they fall into the defiled categories of specialists. At the same time, however, the reimbursements they receive

TABLE VI

	DHOBI													NAI						LOHAR				BARHAI						KUMHAR				
	Chunnalal	Khelawan	Diljhori	Dhanpat	Annunan	Jhagaroo	Ratan	Sarjudai	Buddhu	Dukhi	Parbata	Triloki	Phayadin	Wali Muh'd	Ohmpat	Haricat	Ram Baran	Brijnath	Hajri	Tiri	Ram Udit	Bittal	Ram	Patesa	Shankar	Bhagwandin	Jinky	Jussi	Jawahar	Ramjus	Jhurai	Baijnath	Basanta	Buddhu
Shri Ram Misra	X																X			X										XX				
Sarjuprasad Misra / Chhedi Misra	X																XX			XX										XX				
Ram Babhuti Singh / Lal Singh				X	X									X							X		X			X				X		X		
Mahadev Singh / Ram Narain Singh		X				X											XX			X						XX				X				
Sukhraj Singh / Shiv Datta Singh						XX											XX			X										XX				
Ram Baran Lal / Goku Lal	X					X																								X				
Ram Shankar / Ram Lakhan												XX		XX						X						X				X				
Suraj Bali / Ram Din			X														X			X						X				X	X			
Ram Namaj / Shripat	XX																XX			XX										XX				
Chhedi / Ram Aserey	XX													X			X			X		X				X				XX				
Ram Baran / Ram Baran	X																XX			XX												X		
Ram Baran / Bhagwati															X	X					XX					XX				XX				
Sangam / Ram Pal		X												X	X					X				X	X					XX				
Munesa / Kamta		XX	X											X							X					X				XX				
Jageshwar / Ram Achal		XX												X	X						X					X				XX				
Ram Cullup / Maharaj						XX									X	X				X							X			XX				
Hansraj / Hunnaram														X	X						XX					X	X			XX				X
Surajpal / Chhedi						XX										XX				XX								X	X	XX				
Shri Ram / Chumaroo						XX								XX						XX						X				XX				
Ram Tirat / Sartraj						X		X						X	X					XX						X				XX				
Ram Lakhan / Sarvadin								X						X						XX					X		X			XX				
Bhagwandin / Wali Muhammad						X							X	X						X					X		X						X	
Muhammad Yaqub / Tiri									X			X		X						X								X	X	X				
Ram Udit / Ram Bharosey		X																		X						X				X	X			
Jhinku / Shiv Lal		XX															X			X						X					X			
Basante / Dularey		X		X													XX			XX						X				XX				
Ram Bharosey / Ram Piyarey		X																		X						X				X	X			
Hublal / Anju				X										X						X								X		X		X		
Hittulal / Bipat		X											X					X		X	X							X	X	X	X			
Garibe Das / Damsodin	X											X								X	X			X	X					X				
Ram Bahorey / Jhaggary		X														X				X		X				X				X	X			
Jhaggu / Algu						XX							X							XX								X	X	XX				
Nankhai / Ram Baksh	X													XX			XX			XX						X				XX				

A JAJMANI SYSTEM: STRUCTURE, MAGNITUDE & MEANING 179

include small grants of land, to which they have added a little more through inheritance and rental. Consequently, all are in turn jajman. Shivlal, Basante, and Bipat engage the same washerman as one of the Thakur households. Though their barber is exclusive to them, their blacksmith is Tiri, who has a large elite caste clientele, and their carpenter is the same as that of the two most powerful Thakurs in the community, Ram Babhuti Singh and Mahadev Singh.

The jajmani relationships depicted in Table 6, it should be emphasized, comprise an enormously complex network of intercaste interaction. Theoretically, the variety of jajman-specialist ties among the 70 households of Sherupur and Naktipur, on the one hand, and the 35 households of specialists who serve them, on the other, provide almost infinite opportunities for the establishment of social contacts between persons who would otherwise have no means of approaching one another. Furthermore, the ramifications of the network do not stop with the nine hamlets that are linked as a result of the ties we have described, for the specialists who deal with households in Sherupur and Naktipur have clienteles which reach into still other hamlets. Taken to its logical conclusion, therefore, such a network as this ultimately reaches to the borders of a linguistic region and perhaps to some extent even beyond.

The second kind of evidence in support of the view that jajman status is more a religio-economic category than a social stratum emerges from a careful economic ranking of the 70 households in Sherupur and Naktipur. Each household was ranked according to a common scale on the basis of points allocated as follows:

2 points for each *kachha bigha* (0.4 acres) of land owned;
1 point for each *kachha bigha* of land held on a rental basis;
2 points for each draft animal (bullocks and horses) owned;
1 point for each other farm animal owned, e.g., cows, goats, buffaloes, pigs;
1 point for each Rs 240 per annum of effective cash income from sources other than agriculture.[8]

The resultant scores provide a basis for making a quantitative judgment of each household's level of economic well-being as well as of the extent to which this derives from self-employed farming or from cash realized from other occupations. The purpose was to ascertain whether greater reliance on self-employed farming implies deeper involvement in traditional jajmani ties and whether greater reliance upon a cash income implies lesser involvement with such ties.

The scores range from 255.1 to 1.0 with a mean of 37.5. The rank order of scores does not concern us here, however. What we shall consider is the degree to which economic support depends upon cash income as opposed to farming and the significances of differences which obtain between groupings of households on this basis. Table 7 compares groupings with varying sources of income in terms of their economic relationships with the five sets of specialists. Widows have been excluded from the tabulations because of their very special circumstances.[9]

TABLE 7

Relationship Between Percentage of Economic Score Derived from Cash Incomes and Types of Economic Relationships Maintained With Five Sets of Specialists

Per cent of Score from Cash Income	No. of Households	No. of Grain Payt's	No. of Barter Payt's	Money to Specific Specialist	Money to Available Specialist	Relationships as a Ratio of One Hundred
0 to 5	21	85	—	19	1	81:0:18:1
6 to 25	18	55	1	29	5	51:1:32:6
26 to 50	11	21	17	13	1	40:34:26:1
51 to 100	12	20	5	11	24	33:8:19:40
Total	62	181	23	72	31	60:7:23:10

Table 7 reveals clearly that pure agriculturalists—the category depending only 0 to 5 per cent on cash income—maintain the highest proportion of fully orthodox economic ties with the five sets of specialists. As a grouping they exceed even the Elite-Pure category (see Table 3)—one more indication that jajman-specialist ties do not form a simple hierarchical order.

Indeed, the category of households almost exclusively dependent upon self-employed agriculture includes members of four distinct castes, namely, Brahman, Thakur, Ahir, and Kurmi. All are Twice Born, to be sure, but they span the first three varna and in no sense comprise a single class.

The households of the second category—those who depend on cash incomes for from 6 to 25 percent of their economic support—also exhibit a strong tendency to maintain orthodox jajmani relationships. However, in their case, this necessitates establishing a comparatively large number of the "compromise." traditional ties involving piecework payments to a permanent specialist. Indeed, this category of households manifests a higher proportion of these kinds of reimbursement than does any other. The households of this category are highly variable in material circumstances and ritual status. Seven of them belong to Menial-Impure castes (Kori and Chamar). These are mainly households which, despite their position at the bottom of the social hierarchy, nevertheless possess modest resources through ownership and/or rental of land. With these limited means, and through a variety of economic expedients, they endeavor to approximate as nearly as possible the social patterns of the orthodox elite.

This pattern persists in its essentials in the third category of households—those who derive 26 to 50 per cent of their income from cash sources. The main difference is that artisans, who rely mainly on the exchange of services, predominate at this level. Otherwise, we still find that only a negligible number of specialist services are performed on a wholly non-traditional basis. The urge to maintain orthodox religio-economic status remains strong despite generally low economic scores (all but one being less than 14.0) and heavy dependence upon cash sources for support. Four Kori households, for example, whose respective economic scores are 14.0, 13.5, 5.0, and 4.0, reveal only a single economic relationship in twenty that lies entirely outside the jajmani system with respect to the mode of reimbursement.

Beyond the point where economic support depends preponderantly on agriculture, a marked change in the pattern of economic ties with the five sets of specialists becomes evident. As a rule, households which derive more than 50 per cent of their support from cash incomes are less able or less inclined to maintain orthodox patterns of economic interaction. A single generalization cannot, however, account for all the cases in this category. Not all the households are of Menial-Impure status, although most are, and the exceptions include one Brahman household, that of Shri Ram. Poverty will not suffice as an explanation because this Brahman household is one of the richest in Sherupur, with an economic score of 92.0. It derives support both from land and from a wholesale grain business, which nowadays constitutes its dominant source of livelihood. Yet even such heavy reliance upon an extra-village cash income has not altered the household's determination to preserve orthodox religious and social standing in the community. Its members continue to perform all aspects of Hindu ritual and retain classical economic ties with all of the traditional specialists. Deep involvement in the cash nexus, even on a relatively modern commercial basis, has not in itself led to abandonment of the jajmani system.

Similarly, poverty combined with heavy reliance on cash income does not guarantee that a household will fall outside the jajmani system. Once again the crucial variable is *the degree of investment one cares to make in orthodoxy*. As an illustration I have selected six households from Sherupur-Naktipur which have in common the following facts: (a) that their economic standing is relatively low, (b) that they rely heavily on cash incomes for their support, and (c) that they nevertheless display a highly orthodox pattern of involvement in the jajmani system. Table 8 supplies the pertinent data.

What accounts for the tendency of these six households to manifest such highly orthodox patterns of economic relationships with the five sets of specialists is the fact that all are *bhagat*. This word signifies an intense devotion of God (Bhagwan), which is symbolized in social practice by abstention from eating meat, smoking, and drinking; by the assiduous performance of rituals; and by leading in general a mode of life which we in the West would characterize as puritanical. The expression of this religious fervor in economic terms is achieved by approximating as nearly as possible the status of jajman. For such meagerly endowed households this is not an easy task, but so strong is their motivation that they succeed in their aim to a remarkable extent.

TABLE 8

Economic Structure of Some Selected Low-Income Households, Which Maintain Jajman Status

Head of Household	Caste	Economic Score	Percentage of Income from Cash	Specialist Ratio
Ram Bahore	Kori	2.0	100	4:0:1:0
Algu	Kori	20.9	57	4:0:1:0
Jhagarod Das	Kori	4.0	50	4:0:1:0
Dhamsodin	Kori	14.0	43	4:0:1:0
Sumere	Kori	13.5	41	3:0:1:1
Ram Baran	Murau	13.0	39	4:0:1:0

V

The findings presented here concern a single locality in a particular region of India. It is likely, therefore, that the jajmani system as depicted here will differ in many details of its structure from local manifestations of the phenomenon elsewhere. An important research task still ahead of us is to ascertain the amount of variability that obtains among jajmani systems from locality to locality. The study of regional variations in caste structure and caste ranking by Marriott (1962) is an outstanding illustration of the value of assembling compatible data on a single institution from different parts of India. Among his findings, in fact, is one to the effect that multinucleated villages are far more common in north than in south India. This suggests the possibility that jajmani relationships in south India may be less widely dispersed than they are in places like Sherupur.

Better interregional data should also lead to a more thorough understanding of the sociology of the jajman status. Such data will need to have a historical perspective because we must learn how social change has affected the opportunities of people from different castes to become jajman. In the days when power in rural communities was more unambiguously concentrated in the hands of a dominant caste, whose local position was sanctioned and reinforced by royal decree and royal force, the status of jajman might have been more restricted in its scope. It is conceivable that then a landed aristocracy with elite caste pedigrees were exclusively jajman, whereas specialists, excepting Brahmans, were landless artisans and menials of middle and low caste antecedents. Doubtless pre-modern Indian society more nearly approximated this picture than does the contemporary society because the opportunities for socially approved upward mobility were infinitely less. However, I believe that even in the old social order the jajman status was never confined, even in theory, merely to a landed aristocracy.

Even if we grant that the nonelite castes were unable to be as open in their adoption of social orthodoxy before the modern state was born, it does not necessarily follow that specialists serving high-caste patrons were not themselves jajman as they are today. Inquiries made in Sherupur-Naktipur established the fact that nonelite castes retained the same basic roster of specialists as they do now during the immediately preceding era when the Raja of Ayodhiya reigned over the region.[10] This means that castes who at that time were not entitled to own land, but only to farm it for a share of its income, still found it possible to maintain the jajman status. Only Brahman and Thakur households could own land outright. Such castes as the Ahir, Kurmi, and Murau were technically serfs of the Raja, as were the various artisans and menials in his domain. The early writers who discussed conditions in the pre-independence period of Indian history almost always confined themselves to the elite echelons of the society. This created a precedent for viewing jajmani relationships from the top down and gave rise to the unexamined assumption that jajman status could not be adopted by members of the nonelite castes.

This leads to one final point. Power in Indian society has been won and wielded throughout its long history by a great variety of conquerors, many of whom were not Hindus. The personnel of political hierarchies consequently changed periodically with the vicissitudes of dynastic fortunes. In the seven centuries prior to the coming of British rule, in particular, the ruling classes of the major Indian states were normally Muslim. After the British, the political structure became a melange of competing factions. However, the jajmani system remained unaffected in its underlying characteristics throughout because it did not depend for its existence upon the vicissitudes of the political superstructure; it depended upon the survival of Hinduism. The ruling dynasty might be Muslim or European, and persons who were members of the ruling classes might be jajman as well in their own communities, for many Hindus participated in the political order at all levels no matter who dominated it. But being a jajman and being part of the currently dominant political order were not automatically coterminous. Membership in the political hierarchy was merely one means of achieving a material and power position enabling one to be a jajman if one so desired. It was never the exclusive means. Being a jajman meant being an orthodox rural Hindu whose value system made necessary the engagement of certain specialists. Being a landlord meant being a member of the ruling class, past or present.

Today, when the sanctions for "feudal" status and land tenure are completely undermined in law and the public philosophy, and are fast disappearing, the jajmani system remains viable because, as we have seen, its existence depends primarily on the motivation of the peasantry to practice orthodox Hinduism quite apart from the sources of the wealth which they invest in its practice. As a matter of fact, this has been a source of considerable dismay to modern planners in India, who most heartily wish that a more direct connection existed between the adoption of modern technology, education, medicine, and nationalist ideology and the abandonment of traditional institutions like caste and the jajmani system.

It is this which comparative data, when available, may show. The link between jajman is not a quality like "feudal status" or a "common inclination to exploit the weak" but the mutual wish to practice certain rituals and a way of life necessitating the avoidance of impurity. Within the broad framework of a power differential which makes it possible for some to induce others to perform defiling and demeaning tasks, exploitation is an inevitability up to a point. We see it written in the smaller annual payments which elite caste households make to specialists by comparison with those made by others. But it cannot be exploitation where the jajman and the specialist are of approximately equal status or where, as is common, the specialist is better off than his client. The system, in other words, does not rest upon a simple dichotomy between rich and poor whose implications work themselves out in a self-contained village community. It arises from a religious dichotomy between pure and impure whose implications work themselves out in a complex system of religious and economic relationships embracing, and indeed in large part defining the dimensions of, a locality.

REFERENCES

[1] Since 1954, it has been possible for me to spend a total of 45 months in India. For this opportunity I owe profound debts of gratitude to three generous sources. It was as a Fulbright Student that I was able to make my first field trip to India in 1954-55. My return in 1959-60 was facilitated by a postdoctoral fellowship from the National Science Foundation. Two additional years, from 1960 to 1962, were then made possible by concurrent postdoctoral fellowships from the National Institute of Mental Health.

[2] Not all Brahmans are priests. Indeed, these constitute only a small minority. The majority, who may be called "secular Brahmans," practice agricultural proprietorship, shopkeeping, and other occupations that are religiously sanctioned alternatives to priesthood.

[3] "Permanent" is a relative term here. It would perhaps be more appropriate to say that permanence is what is striven for in these relationships. In actual fact, changes are made from time to time by both patrons and specialists in consequence of quarrels over rates of reimbursement, clashes of personality, competitive bidding for the services of a specialist, etc.

[4] A leading Rajput family in Sherupur say the following may be given to the Pandit: (1) seven paseri (28 pounds) of grain at plowing time as recompense for killing living organisms in the soil; (2) 10 per cent of the dowry of any marriage he helps to arrange; (3) one dhoti (cotton garment worn by men), one blouse, and one pair of sandals when a woman in the household dies; (4) one dhoti, one shirt, and one pair of sandals when a man in the household dies; (5) twelve free meals (one each month for a year) after any death in the household; (6) a few coins whenever an astrological reading is obtained.

[5] In an earlier paper (Gould 1958), I erroneously stated that the Thakur caste of Sherupur was part of the Raghubansi clan.

[6] Beidelman (1959) has argued that specialists fare better in the power structure the better organized they are. However, if average remunerations are any criterion, this may not always be the case. In Sherupur's locality, the washerman caste has one of the most active caste panchayats (councils), whereas the carpanters and ironsmiths, have very weak ones. Yet, as Table 2 demonstrates, the latter two castes are better paid than are the washermen. Apparently demography can sometimes override politics, because it would appear that the position enjoyed by the Barhai and Lohar stems from their extremely small numbers.

[7] According to Mathur (1958: 51-52), who has published one of the best discussions of this pointe "...agriculture is largely considered to be 'caste free'. There are, no doubt, 'cultivater castes'...but agriculture is in no sense a caste monopoly, and all castes, down to the very lowest untouchables may practice cultivation...Agriculture may thus be regarded as an 'open' occupation which could be and was pursued by any caste irrespective of its ritual status and position in the caste hierarchy."

[8] The assumption that a unit of land held on rental is only half as valuable to the cultivator as the same quantity owned outright is based upon an estimate that the cost of renting land normally absorbs about half of its income. "Effective cash income" refers to take-home pay. Cash earned for work in the village or through a job involving daily, short-distance commuting is assemed to be 100 per cent "effective" in this sense. However, where an individual is working permanently outside the locality and contributes to the household by sending money periodically, the assumption is made that only 10 per cent of the money earned by persons with menial occupations and about 30 per cent of that earned by persons with "white collar" occupations actually reaches the family in the village. A further assumption is that Rs. 240 per annum is, everything considered, about as valuable on the average as ownership of a *kachha bigha* of cultivable land. It is conceded that various other criteria for gauging economic standing might have been employed, and perhaps in the future other combinations may be fruitfully tried (cf. Lewis and Barnouw 1956). The criteria adopted, however, seemed adequate for our purposes as well as consonant with our ethnographic observations.

[9] When compelled to live alone or to act as household heads, in the absence of adult males, widows find it virtually impossible to maintain levels of economic well-being and religious purity sufficient to permit any meaningful utilization of the jajmani system. The category of widows contains one Kayastha, two Ahir, one Kori, and one Chamar. The ratios for their relationships with the five sets of specialists is 3:0:7:90. In other words these women engage the services of washermen, barbers, potters, carpenters, and blacksmiths almost exclusively on a cash-as-needed basis 90 per cent of the time.

[10] The Raja of Ayodhiya ruled over an extensive domain between the Great Uprising in 1857 and the abolition of landlordism in 1947 after India won her independence from Great Britain.

BIBLIOGRAPHY

Baden-Powell, B.H. 1896. The Indian Village Community, London.
Bailey, F.G. 1958. Caste and the Economic Frontier. London.
———, 1960. Tribe, Caste and Nation. Manchester.
Beidelman, T. 1959. A Comparative Study of the Jajmani System. Ann Arbor: Assn for Asian Studies.
Bennett, J.W., and L. Despres. 1960. Kinship and Instrumental Activities: A Theoretical inquiry. American Anthropologist 62:254-267.
Berreman, G.D. 1962. Caste and Economy in the Himalayas. Economic Development and Cultural Change 8:386-394.
Bougle, C. 1908. Essais sur les regimes des castes, Paris.
Cohn, B.S. 1959a. Madhopur Revisited. Economic Weekly II (Special Number): 963-966.
———, 1959b. Some Notes on Law and Social Change in North India. Economic Development and Cultural Change 8:79-93.
Dumont, L., and D. Pocock. 1958. Commented Summary of the First Part of Bougle's Essais. Contributions to Indian Sociology, ed., L. Dumont and D. Pocock 2:31-44.
Foster, G.M. 1958. What is Folk Culture? American Anthropologist, 55:159-173.
Gould, H.A. 1958. The Hindu Jajmani System: A Case of Economic Particularism. Southwestern Journal of Anthropology 14:428-437.
———, 1960. The Micro-Demography of Marriages in a North Indian Area Southwestern journal of Anthropology 10:476-491.
Harper, B.P., 1958. Two Systems of Economic Exchange in Village India. American Anthropology 61:766-778.
Hocart, A.M. 1950. Caste, London.
Jaffri, S.N.S. 1951. The History and Status of Landlords, and Tenants in the United Provinces (India). Allahabad.
Kolenda, P.M. 1963. Toward a Model of the Jajmani System. Human Organization 22:11-31.
Lewis, O., and V. Barnouw. 1956. Aspects of Land Tenure and Economics in a North Indian Village. Economic Development and Cultural Change 4:279-302.
Majumdar, D.N. 1960. Book Review of T. Beidelman, A Comparative Study of the Jajmani System, Man 66:80.
Marriort, Mckim, 1959. Intersectional and Attributional Theories of Caste Ranking. Man in India 59:92-107.
———, 1960. Caste Ranking and Community Structure in Five Regions of India and Pakistan. Deccan. College Monograph Series 23:1-75.

Mathur, R.S. 1958. Caste and Occupation in a Malwa Village. Eastern Anthropologist 12 47-61.
Mayer, A.C. 1958, The Dominant Caste in a Region of Central India. Southwestern Journal of Anthropology 14:407-427.
———, 1960. Caste and Kinship in Central India. London.
Miller, E.J. 1954. Caste and Territory in Malabar. American Anthropologist 56:410-420.
Moreland, W.H. (n.d.). The Agrarian System of Moslem India. Allahabad.
Mukerjee, R.K. 1961. A note on Village as Unit for Studies of Rural Society. Eastern Anthropologist 14:3-17.
Opler, M. and R.D. Singh. 1948. The Division of Labor in an Indian Village. A Reader in General Anthropology, ed., C.S. Coon, pp. 464-496. New York.
Orenstein, H., 1962. Explantation of Function in the Interpretation of Jajmani. Southwestern Journal of Anthropology 18:302-316.
Pocock, D.,1965. Notes on Jajmani Relationships. Contributions to Indian Sociology. ed., L. Dumont and D. Pocock 6: 78 95.
Redfield, R. 1941. The Folk Culture of Yucatan. Chicago.
Wiser, W. 1956. The Hindu Jajmani System. Lucknow.

Index

Achievement-oriented stratification 76
Alexander the Great 2, 30
American South 45
Aryans 85
Ascription-oriented stratification 75, 76, 78, 80
Ashoka, Emperor 86, 92

Badaga tribe 122, 123, 125-131
Baden-Powell, B.H. 151, 167
Bailey, F.G. 3, 4
Bali 91,
Barbers (Nai) 158, 163
Beidelman, T. 161, 174, 187
Berreman, Gerald D. 22, 51, 53, 154-156
Bhangi caste 163
Bougle, Celestin 6
Brahmanas 14, 38, 47, 113, 115, 116, 187
Breeks, J.W. 130
British rule 185
Bronze-age 79, 80
Buddhism 10, 87, 90-96, 100

Carpenters (Barhai) 158
Caste differentiation 52
Caste endogamy 169
Caste system 2, 114, 136, 146
Caste system of India 45

Ceylon 91, 92
Chamar 161, 162
Childe, V. Gordon 34, 35, 39
China 87, 94, 96, 99
Chinese civilization 88
Christianity 67, 92, 93
'Clean' castes 136, 139
'Clean' occupations 136, 153, 154
Colonialism 97
Confusianism 95
'Considerations' 140, 142, 146, 147
Crooke, W. 93

Davis, Kinglsey 136
Dharma 17
Division of labor 135, 136
Dumont, L. 5, 10, 11, 12, 19, 50, 53
Durkheim, E. 104-107

Economic relationships 159, 160, 175, 181
Emeneau, M.B. 128
Esterik, Van 25

Fertile Crescent 2, 3, 34, 43, 45, 52, 68
Field labor 164
Five-year plans 59

INDEX 191

Fox, R. 122, 124, 127-131
'Functional interchangeability' 162

Ghurye, G.S 81, 93
Gould, H.A 173, 187
Grain payments, 157, 158
Greece 97

Harkness, H.A. 128, 131
Harper, E.D. 51, 155
'Hereditary specialization' 154
Hertz, Robert 25
Hindu and Southern system 51
Hindu caste system 14
Hinduism 13, 68, 80, 110
Hindu Jajmani system 49
Hindu sacred law 111, 112
Hocart, A.M. 7-9, 50, 91
Hough, J. 127
Hsuan Tsang 31
Hume, Robert Ernest 25,
Hutton, J.H. 32, 33, 83

Inden, R. 22
Independence 59
Industrialization 55-57, 60, 61, 76
Industrial revolution 54, 68
Indus Valley Civilization 13, 34, 45, 84
Intransitive and *transitive* pollution (*See also* Pollution) 112
Irula tribe 124-126, 129

Jaffri, S.N.S. 156
Jajmani relationship 142, 145, 165, 180, 182, 185

Jojmani system 8, 116, 117, 123, 126, 128, 132, 139, 140, 146, 149, 152, 154, 159, 169, 172-178, 183-186
Jajmani system in Sherupur 146,
Jajman purjan ties 143, 144, 164
Jajman status 184, 185
Japan 88, 89
Jatis 7

Kahl, J.A. 61
Kanishka 87
Karma 17, 18
Karma-samsara 16
Kinship system 138, 140
Klass, M. 23
Kolenda, P. 161, 166, 168
Kori caste 161
Kota tribe 123-126, 128-130
Kshatriya 39, 114, 115, 117
Kurumba tribe 124-126, 128, 129, 131

Leach, Edmund 1, 21, 33
Levi-strauss, Claude 106, 107, 108
Linton, Ralph 39

Mabbett, I.W. 25
Marriott, M. 22, 138, 144, 184
Marshall, W.E. 130
Marx, K. 57, 58
Mathur, R.S. 188
Maya 17, 47
Modernization 58
Modern occupations 54
Moreland, W.H. 152
Muslim agrarian system 152

Nadel, S.F. 4, 24, 39, 40, 44, 98
Nilgiri Hills 112, 121
Nilgiri *jajmani* system 124-126, 130-132
Nilgiri tribes 131 ff.
Nonindustrial societies 76, 79
Nuba clans 44, 98

Occupational categories 36, 61
Occupational roles 37, 38, 84
Occupational specialization 161
Once Born 18, 19
Opler, M. 163
Orenstein, H. 108, 111, 112, 174
Outcaste groups 82, 83

Pandharipande, Rajeshwari 26
Passin, H. 23, 81, 82, 89, 111, 136
Payments for the services 156
Pocock, D.F. 5, 50, 174, 176
Pollution problem 49, 129
Polynesia 96
Potters (Kumhar) 158
Preindustrial state system 40, 42
Priest and 'contrapriest' 115
Purjans 119, 120, 125, 139, 142
Purity/pollution opposition 109
'Purusha myth' 13
Purwa Mimamsa 14
Pusalker, A. D. 46

Radcliffe-Brown, 107

Rajput 62
Rebirth 17
Rig Veda 13, 38
Rivers, W.H.R. 128, 130
Roger, Abraham 32
Rome 97
Rowe, J.H. 156

Sahlins, M.D. 29
Samsara 14
Sansom 88
Schweitzer, A. 109
Sheffield 58
Sherupur 137, 140-145, 147, 149, 150, 169, 176
Sherupur-Naktipur 151, 152, 154, 156, 162, 168, 169, 170, 174, 177, 180, 183, 185
Singh, R.D. 163
Sirkanda village 155
Sjoberg, Gideon 41
Social orthodoxy 158
Social stratification 39, 74
South Asia 50
Southern social system 52
Southern United States 53
Specialists 172, 173
Srinivas, M.N. 21, 120
Strabo 31
Sudras 19, 39, 114, 115
Swanson, G. E. 109

Tailors (Darzi) 164
Taoism 95
Theravada 86
Tibet 89
Toda tribe 122, 125, 127, 128-130
Totemism 107

INDEX

Twice Born 18, 19

'Unclean' castes 136, 139
Unclean occupations 136
Untouchables 73, 81, 90

Vaisya 39, 69, 114, 115, 117
Varna 13, 20, 113, 116
'Village, the' 166
Von Furer-Haimendorf 24

Warner, W. Lloyd 29
Washermen (Dhobi) 158
Weber, Max 6
Wiser, William 8, 137, 140, 146, 149, 151, 152, 156, 167, 168
Wheeler, Sir Mortimer 45
Wolf, Eric 37
Woodcock, George 23